101
LEARNING AND
DEVELOPMENT
TOOLS

Essential
Techniques
for Creating,
Delivering
and Managing
Effective Training

Kenneth Fee

101
Learning and
Development
Tools

101
Learning and Development Tools

Essential techniques for creating, delivering and managing effective training

Kenneth Fee

KoganPage

LONDON PHILADELPHIA NEW DELHI

First published in Great Britain and the United States in 2011 by Kogan Page Limited

120 Pentonville Road	1518 Walnut Street, Suite 1100	4737/23 Ansari Road
London N1 9JN	Philadelphia PA 19102	Daryaganj
United Kingdom	USA	New Delhi 110002
www.koganpage.com		India

© Kenneth Fee, 2011

The right of Kenneth Fee to be identified as the author of this work has been asserted by him in accordance with the Copyright, Designs and Patents Act 1988.

ISBN   978 0 7494 6108 9
E-ISBN 978 0 7494 6109 6

British Library Cataloguing-in-Publication Data

A CIP record for this book is available from the British Library.

Library of Congress Cataloging-in-Publication Data

Fee, Kenneth.
    101 learning and development tools : essential techniques for creating, delivering, and managing effective training / Kenneth Fee.
        p. cm.
    ISBN 978-0-7494-6108-9 -- ISBN 978-0-7494-6109-6   1. Organizational learning.   2. Employees-
-Training of.   3. Computer-based instruction.   I. Title.   II. Title: One hundred one learning and development tools.   III. Title: One hundred and one learning and development tools.
    HD58.82.F44 2011
    658.3'124--dc22
                                                                                        2011010655

Typeset by Graphicraft Ltd, Hong Kong
Printed and bound in India by Replika Press Pvt Ltd

CONTENTS

LIST OF FIGURES

LIST OF TABLES

ABOUT THE AUTHOR

Kenneth Fee has worked in learning and development for 25 years, as a trainer, consultant, manager and writer, among other roles. He has an MA degree in social science, an MBA, certificates in training and in assessment, and a professional diploma in training management. He is a chartered fellow of CIPD and a fellow of CMI.

His previous books include *A Guide to Management Development Techniques* and *Delivering E-Learning*, both published by Kogan Page. Since 2007, he has written a blog at **http://learnforeverblog.blogspot.com**.

He lives in Lanarkshire, Scotland, United Kingdom, with his wife and son.

ACKNOWLEDGEMENTS

This work contains reference to a large number of tools and techniques originating from other sources. Thanks are due to the following (or their estates, where applicable) and their publishers: Malcolm Knowles for his theory of andragogy, Stewart Hase for his theory of heutagogy, Roger W Sperry for left versus right brain, George A Kelly for his repertory grid, Benjamin Bloom for his taxonomy of learning domains, David A Kolb for his experiential learning cycle, Peter Honey and Alan Mumford for their learning styles model, Colin Rose for his learning styles model and for accelerated learning, Joseph Luft and Harry Ingham for the Johari window, Michael Porter for his value chain, Peter Senge for his fifth discipline and its application to learning cultures and the learning organization, Mike Pedler, John Burgoyne and Tom Boydell for their definition of a learning organization, Daniel Goleman for emotional intelligence, Howard Gardner for his multiple intelligences, Richard Bandler and John Grinder for neuro-linguistic programming, Mick Cope for his structural model of the management of knowledge, Andy Cross for the talent web, David Clutterbuck for his learning alliances, Bob Aubrey and Paul Cohen for their five skills of mentoring, Roberto Moretti for his practice-made-perfect system, Reginald Revans for action learning, Etienne Wenger for communities of practice, Donald Kirkpatrick for his four levels of evaluation, Kaliym Islam for his application of Six Sigma to training and development, and all the authors and publishers whose works are cited in this book. Thanks as well to the Boston Consulting Group for their growth share matrix, the Chartered Institute of Personnel and Development for their partnership of learning model, General Electric and McKinsey for the GE nine box model, Motorola Incorporated for Six Sigma, NHS Education for Scotland for the diamond model of quality assuring continuous professional development, Volunteer Development Scotland for VSkills, and the Wizards Network for the chocolate factory.

The author would also like to thank the following for their suggestions and advice: Hannah Berry, Peter Farr, Karen Fee, Elizabeth Holden, Lindsay Officer, Martyn Sloman, Matthew Smith, and everyone who responded to discussion topics initiated in groups on LinkedIn, and followed posts on the learnforever blog, **http://learnforeverblog.blogspot.com**.

Introduction

Lindsay's story

Lindsay didn't always want to work in human resources; very few young people do. Her interest in business was first sparked at school, when she took part in a young entrepreneurs' competition, in the role of deputy personnel director, but it was only after graduating with an English degree, qualified for nothing but teaching or academia, that she reviewed her vocational options and chose to study for a postgraduate Master's degree in HR.

On qualifying, she lacked experience, having undertaken only a short student placement in an HR generalist role, but after temping in administrative positions for a few months she was able to secure a position as training and development coordinator for an oil industry support company. Lindsay's responsibilities included administering training courses for 600 offshore oil workers, and occasionally helping with administration in employee relations issues.

This gave her a start, and she was able to move on, after two years, to the post of HR and training manager for a large hotel, part of a well-known chain. This was mainly a generalist role, beset by an industry sector problem of recruiting low-skilled employees, earning minimum wage, to jobs where they rarely stayed long. Lindsay found herself undertaking a lot of recruitment, managing staff shortages – even to the extent of helping out with waitressing – and handling many disciplinary procedures. Despite some interesting work in training and in health and safety, Lindsay found the long working hours and lack of opportunity to develop staff frustrating, and within three years made another move, this time to a much better role.

The post of HR adviser in the employee development team of a local authority proved to offer a much more varied range of work, and four years on she still holds this position. Her responsibilities include considering development needs, sourcing training from external providers, delivering face-to-face training in subjects like team building, performance management and leading change, and writing e-learning courses.

Lindsay enjoys using her interpersonal skills in a more positive way, meeting people's needs and maintaining a customer focus. She relishes opportunities to exercise her creativity when designing training courses and online learning. She is a little concerned about the decay of her generalist skills and up-to-date knowledge of employment law, as she concentrates more and more on learning and development. And she finds her career very demanding. But overall she still describes HR as her 'dream job' and maintains she would recommend it to anyone.

What follows is aimed primarily at people like Lindsay.

The importance of learning and development

If you're reading this book, you probably already think learning and development are important. We commence from that premise.

Anyone who stops to think about it for more than a few seconds is bound to conclude that learning is an important part of life, essential to human progress, to individual development from infancy onwards, and to the way groups, organizations and societies improve themselves and fulfil their goals.

Learning is a broad concept, referring to many different things, but when we pair it with development that means we are talking about occupational learning, or learning in the sphere of work and organizations. That's the meaning of learning and development in this book.

Learning is both very simple and very complex. It is simple in that we all do it all the time, as instinctively as breathing, and although we may be aware of what we're learning, we often don't think about how we're learning or what is helping us to learn. It is complex in that we understand surprisingly little about the process; there are competing theories of how the brain works, and how our conscious mind acquires and processes new information, evaluates it and applies it. The last bit, application, is of great importance when it comes to learning for work.

Development has many different meanings, but in the context of learning is about how we apply learning to benefit ourselves (individual and team development) and our organizations (organizational development).

When we plan learning at work, we are trying to harness the simple urge to learn, and organize the learning so that we direct our efforts to the goals of our organizations. We try to plan the learning, to create the most efficient and effective support processes, and to ensure we can record what happens so that we can repeat what works well and learn from what doesn't.

Over many years, a science has developed: not a very precise science, but one that acknowledges successes in helping people learn for work, and one that yields an array of tools and techniques that improve our chances of emulating those successes. This science is what we, rather clumsily, refer to as learning and development. Some prefer the terms 'human resource development', 'employee development' and 'training and development', all of which essentially mean the same thing.

The need for a guide

This book is conceived as a practical guide for those who wish to manage other people's learning as well as their own. It is not a work of theory, or academia, although it cites the theoretical sources of each tool and offers suggestions to the reader for further investigation, even academic study. Instead, it is intended to complement works of theory about learning and development, as listed at the end of this introduction. It is a working manual for learning and development managers, or trainers, or anyone who needs to design and deliver a learning intervention, or support learning in some way, or manage learning activities.

The further reading list at the end of this introduction cites a number of more academic studies, and general readers on learning and development, which complement the scope of this work and in some instances offer deeper insights.

Theory and practice are closely related: theory informs practice, and practice in turn informs theory. The tools in this book are good examples of this in action: in each case, the accumulated experience of practice is distilled into a tool, and that tool then becomes the theory guiding future practice. These tools remain valid until practice disproves their relevance and demands their adaptation or the creation of new tools.

And yet the sheer number of available tools can be bewildering, and almost defies classification. This book seeks to address this problem, by listing, describing and analysing some of the most common and useful tools, and placing them in a context.

This should be especially useful to relatively new learning and development practitioners. The first time I had to design a course, in first-line management, I worried that I didn't have enough resources. I knew my subject, from reading and from personal experience, but I lacked confidence that I carried enough authority with my learners. So I searched for other sources of authority, and purchased two or three videos and a battery of self-assessment instruments. The effect of this was to bombard the learners with extra information, and somewhat overload the course; with hindsight, a better approach would have been to focus in on the specific needs of the learners, and design activities that would have better met their needs. I would have greatly appreciated a guide such as this, had it existed.

For more experienced learning and development practitioners, who already confidently use an array of their favourite tools, this book offers the opportunity to consider other options, similar or related tools, and the chance to refresh their thinking about the tools they currently use. Perhaps it could challenge assumptions about the way tools are used at present, and point to new ways of working. At the very least, it should provide reassurance about tried, tested and effective approaches.

In a wider context, the gathering of these tools into this collection affords an opportunity to step back and consider how this body of theory and practice really works, and how it affects the way we do things. From the study of evolution, we know that the formation and development of ideas and skills are critical to how humankind – indeed, all conscious species – moves forward, and that humankind has always applied its ideas and skills to develop tools. In this context, learning is the means whereby we accomplish goals and achieve progress, and we learn by using tools.

The meaning of tools

When any do-it-yourself is being done around our house, it's more likely to be my wife who takes it on. But, on the rare occasions when I attempt something, I usually start by looking for the right tool in the tool box. It's tempting – not to say trite – to draw an analogy with my profession and claim that I take the same approach to any learning and development problem. However, the metaphor of the tool box, tool kit or tool bag is one of the most overused, and perhaps the most clichéd, not just for learning and development professionals, but for managers in many business disciplines.

The truth is it's an oversimplification, not least because it's not easy to reach a shared understanding of what we mean by tools in this context.

When I undertook research for this book, I found it hard to get fellow professionals to recognize what I wanted to focus on. Some people thought I was looking for the activities and exercises they deploy when facilitating courses; others wanted to talk about the proprietary products or services they buy or sell in the learning marketplace; still more highlighted broader concepts like questioning techniques, or promoting self-motivation. In their mind, all of these disparate things were 'tools'.

When I asked people to tell me about their favourite learning and development tools, I frequently attracted responses about two different kinds of tools beyond the scope of my enquiry, neither of which is covered in this book. First, some respondents sought to promote the products and services they sell or have a stake in, and while many of these have merit I have tried to avoid detailing them, preferring instead to discuss generic tools, for example psychometric instruments in general, not the Myers–Briggs Type Indicator in particular. Secondly, other respondents offered their favoured tools for supporting subject-specific learning interventions, such as Belbin's team roles as a tool for supporting team-building training. Again, these are not included, as I have tried to concentrate on tools that may be deployed to manage or support any learning intervention, regardless of its content, subject or discipline.

In addition, I've tried to avoid aids to thinking that could be deployed as learning and development tools, but also have a much wider application, such as SWOT analysis, brain storming, mind mapping, PEST analysis or lateral thinking. Valuable though these are, if I'd included all of these it would have proved impossible to restrict this book to 101 entries.

Many suggestions I received were for tools for delivering training in a classroom-type situation. Most of these were too specific to include, but I have tried to describe categories or clusters of tools, such as icebreakers. Inevitably, this has led to the part of the book dealing with implementing learning containing the largest number of entries.

By casting the net across my network of contacts and online groups, I attracted responses from all over the world: I hope the catch yielded is of global relevance, but I must acknowledge my own locus and national perspective. I am British, and my entire career, both as a writer and as a learning and development professional, has been spent in Britain, apart from a handful of short work trips to Europe and North America. I don't apologize for my inevitably British focus, but I hope readers from other countries can accept that my examples tend to draw on that experience, and yet still find the tools useful.

My research elicited the views of a wide range of contacts and invited contributions via online discussion groups; I've completed an extensive literature review, and drawn on 25 years of experience in learning and development. But there are still bound to be useful tools that I have omitted – this book can't possibly claim to be comprehensive. Nevertheless, I hope it's covered many of the most popular tools and given a reasonable account of them.

Who this book is for

Most medium-to-large organizations employ someone whose main role is to help other people learn: this person may be called a learning and development manager, or a training manager, or an employee development manager, or something like that. In smaller organizations, this role may be part of the remit of the human resources manager or personnel manager. If you work in any of these roles, this book is for you.

There is also a growing body of specialists in organization development, in change management, in talent management and development, and in skills utilization and resourcing. If you work in one of these roles, this book should be useful to you too.

But learning and development is not just the preserve of a few key roles within organizations. Two trends illustrate this: one is for devolving of responsibility to line managers, and the other is for outsourcing. In respect of the first trend, increasingly managers with quite different operational responsibilities are expected to include within their remit responsibility for managing the learning of their subordinates; given their lack of specialized knowledge or training in learning, these managers need this book more than most. And, in respect of the second trend, outside the organization there are many providers of learning and development services, including freelance trainers and consultants, who need this book too.

Smaller organizations can rarely afford the luxury of a learning and development professional, or even a human resources manager. For general managers of these organizations, or specialists in other disciplines, a reference book like this should be invaluable.

Then there is the formal education sector, where staff of colleges and universities are constantly approached to help organizations with learning and development. It is hoped that these staff will also find this book helps them fulfil their role.

These categories represent a crude map of who does what in learning and development, but if you've read this far, and your own role doesn't seem to fit any of these classifications, all this shows is the limitations of the model – if you've read this far and you're still interested, clearly the book is relevant to you.

How to use this book

This book is divided into 101 entries, each following a standard format. This format is shown in Figure I.1.

FIGURE I.1 Format of entries

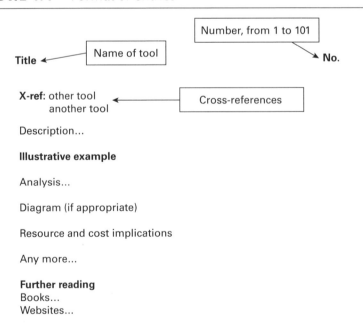

The first tool is the learning and development cycle, which is the keystone of the construct, and the basis of everything that follows. My contention is that the learning and development cycle is the single most important tool used by learning and development practitioners and that all of the other tools that follow may be classified into the four stages of the cycle. Thus, the learning and development cycle becomes the framework for the contents of the subsequent chapters.

There are four parts, corresponding to the four phases of the learning and development cycle. Part 1 features tools that may be used to facilitate learning needs analysis; Part 2 features tools that may be used to facilitate the planning of learning and development; Part 3 features tools that may be used when implementing learning; and Part 4 features tools that may be used when evaluating learning and development.

This cycle is sometimes also known by other names, notably the 'systematic training cycle', and for some it is too systematic. The fiercest criticism of the cycle is that it is too rigid, compartmentalizing thinking and discouraging creative solutions to problems. But the cycle is only as inflexible or as mechanistic as you wish it to be: it can offer a useful starting point, but not necessarily the entire blueprint, for the application of learning and development. The cycle is one way to start thinking about learning and development, and as such helps classify the tools in this book. Readers can make their own choices about which tools to use, and where and when to use them.

This book may be read from start to finish as a linear narrative, or it may be consulted as a reference manual. Each tool is cross-referenced to others that it is related to, and so it is possible to conduct a different sort of journey through the book, starting at your first point of interest and then exploring related themes via the cross-references. I hope it's the sort of book that stays handily placed on the desk or shelf, to be opened and dipped into when the need arises.

Very few of the tools in this book are original – no more than a handful are of my own devising. The great majority are well-known, established tools that have been in use for many years. I believe all of the original sources and authors have been identified and credited, and I apologize for any inadvertent omission. The way they have been explained is mine, and that means I should also apologize to anyone who feels I have not done justice to their particular tool. All of the opinions expressed in this book are mine, unless specifically attributed to others.

FURTHER READING

As in the rest of this book, the list of further reading is merely a selection of suggestions, but as this is the introduction this list is a bit longer than those that follow. There are many references in the works in this list to the tools that populate this book, and so this may be viewed as a 'master list' to refer back to, especially for tools where there is a dearth of dedicated publications. It is also worth bearing in mind that search engines like Google and online encyclopedias like Wikipedia yield a lot of returns on the tools.

Armstrong, M (2009) *Armstrong's Handbook of Human Resource Management Practice*, Kogan Page, London

Hargreaves, P and Jarvis, P (1998) *The Human Resource Development Handbook*, Kogan Page, London

Harrison, R (2009) *Learning and Development*, CIPD, London

Landale, A (ed) (1999) *Gower Handbook of Training and Development*, Gower, Aldershot

Reid, M *et al* (2004) *Human Resource Development: Beyond training interventions*, CIPD, London

Stewart, J (1999) *Employee Development Practice*, FT Prentice Hall, Harlow

Walton, J (1999) *Strategic Human Resource Development*, FT Prentice Hall, Harlow

Wilson, J (2005) *Human Resource Development: Learning and training for individuals and organizations*, Kogan Page, London

http://hr-inform.cipd.co.uk/, an online subscription service from CIPD

http://www.astd.org/, the website of the American Society for Training and Development (ASTD)

http://www.businessballs.com/, an online reference source for business concepts and tools; the sections on human resources and personal development are especially relevant

http://www.cipd.co.uk, the website of the Chartered Institute of Personnel and Development (CIPD)

http://www.trainingjournal.com/, a print and online journal

http://www.trainingzone.co.uk/, an online community

The learning and development cycle

X-REF TOOLS

The learning and development cycle is arguably the single most useful tool for learning and development, and a good starting point for understanding all of the other tools, as it provides a frame of reference. It breaks down learning and development activities into four, sometimes more, phases, and explains how they follow a natural, recurring sequence or cycle. This is illustrated in Figure 0.1.

The idea behind the cycle is that the manager responsible should: identify and analyse the learning needs of the job – or skill, or employee, or work team, or organization – under consideration; use that analysis to plan, design and prepare for an appropriate learning intervention; implement that intervention, perhaps by commissioning or delivering a course or facilitating some work-based learning; and then assess and review the effectiveness of the learning intervention in order to ascertain whether any further learning is needed, which brings us back to the beginning of what is really a continuous cycle.

A more detailed breakdown of the four phases might yield a longer list such as:

- Identify learning needs.
- Analyse those learning needs.
- Clarify learning objectives.
- Determine a strategy to meet those objectives.

FIGURE 0.1   The learning and development cycle

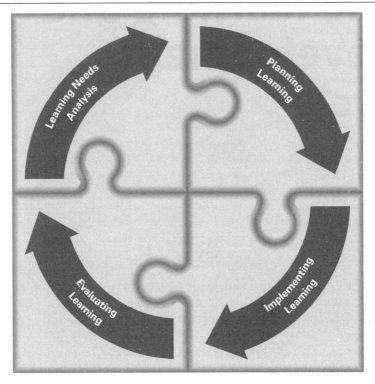

- Plan an appropriate learning intervention.
- Design the learning intervention.
- Prepare for the learning intervention.
- Deliver the learning intervention.
- Support learners through the intervention.
- Measure learner satisfaction.
- Assess the learning outcomes.
- Evaluate the effectiveness of the learning intervention.

The cycle is a reliable tool to use when considering any issue that includes, or may include, a learning need, as it helps break down consideration of the issue into its distinct logical parts.

Some, especially US, sources describe the cycle as the basis of 'instructional systems design', and this leads some critics (eg Köster, 2002) to decry the cycle as *too* systematic. This really just amounts to a sensible warning not to be too constrained by the formula of the cycle. Salomon's related idea (2010) is that all systems – indeed all tools – should be subordinate to ensuring that learners are in the correct frame of mind and are motivated

Illustrative example

A simple illustration of this may be made in a service company's customer care centre. The company may have found, in measuring customer satisfaction by contract renewals, that a lower percentage of customers are being retained in comparison to those of its competitors. This identifies a problem in need of a solution, and analysis may show that better questioning by customer service centre operatives could be that solution (*phase one*). The learning manager could devise a coaching programme (*phase two*), where more experienced and successful operatives listen in on calls by their less experienced colleagues, and then discuss with them where they could improve their questioning (*phase three*). The coaches log the issues they have discussed, and these are collated to track improvements in performance. The key metric for the company is whether contract renewals then rise (*phase four*), and if they do, all else being equal, then the programme may be deemed a success and maintained at least until contract renewals exceed those of their competitors.

to engage with learning. Again, this contextualizes, but does not refute, the value of the cycle.

A more searching critique is that the starting point of the cycle, needs analysis, is too narrow, and should instead be replaced with the organization's objectives or strategy. This critique holds that learning and development practitioners have been too focused on their own function and have taken insufficient heed of the wider implications for their organizations. This may be true in some instances, but again fails to refute the cycle, as long as the needs analysis is itself strategic and fits within the organization's strategy. The critique amounts to a shift in emphasis for one phase of the cycle, as in the version adopted for the United Kingdom's Investors in People standard (see 'Further reading').

There are resource and cost implications for many of the tools in this book, but the only such considerations for the cycle are the time and effort required by the manager responsible, and all other people brought into the process. This should not be underestimated, but this is a tool that should be usable by any manager responsible for learning, without any significant cost or resource barriers.

FURTHER READING

Biech, E (2005) The training cycle, Ch 3 in *Training for Dummies*, Wiley, Hoboken, NJ
Craig, M (1994) *Analysing Learning Needs*, Gower, Aldershot

Dixon, N (1999) *The Organizational Learning Cycle: How we can learn collectively*, Gower, Aldershot

Donovan, P and Townsend, J (2004) *The Training Needs Analysis Pocketbook*, Management Pocketbooks, Alresford

Köster, M (2002) Human resource development: the limitations of the systematic training cycle (essay), Grin, Munich

Salomon, H (2010) *What's Training without Motivation? Analysis of the training cycle by focusing on motivational aspects*, VDM, Saarbrücken

http://cpd.conted.ox.ac.uk/lnat/the_learning_cycle.php, University of Oxford Department of Continuing Education (accessed August 2010)

http://www.investorsinpeople.co.uk/, featuring the IiP framework derived from the learning and development cycle

http://www.ocr.org.uk/download/kd/ocr_10173_kd_fact.pdf, Oxford, Cambridge and RSA Examinations (accessed August 2010)

http://www.rics.org/site/scripts/documents_info.aspx?documentID=807, Royal Institution of Chartered Surveyors (accessed August 2010)

PART ONE
Learning needs analysis

This part of the book considers a range of 27 tools that contribute to learning needs analysis.

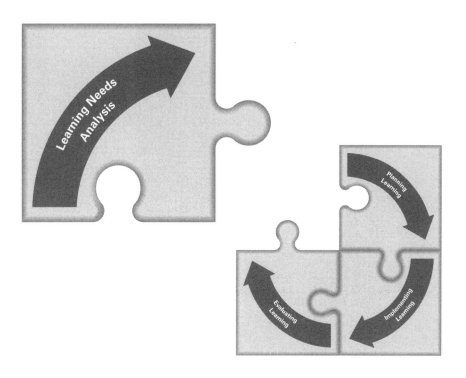

Understanding learning, development, education and training

02

The most elementary tools we have available to us in learning and development are words themselves: the language we use helps us better understand what we are dealing with and helps us better communicate ideas. Rather than simply assuming definitions of common terms, we can benefit from developing a deeper, and hopefully shared, understanding of what the language of learning and development really means.

People often confuse the most common terms, the fundamentals, and so it helps if we can strive for a shared understanding of them. Essentially, learning and development are things that learners do; they are about acquiring knowledge, skills and capabilities. 'Education' and 'training' are terms for the inputs to learning and development provided by teachers, trainers and others, including teaching, training, instruction and coaching.

In my 2001 book *A Guide to Management Development Techniques*, I challenged this orthodoxy, and offered an alternative classification, in which each of these four terms is a subset of a broader term: training is one part of development, which in turn is one part of education, which in turn is one part of learning. I have since relented, and accepted the more common approach, which puts learning and development on the learners' side of the equation, and education and training on the teachers' and trainers' side.

Whatever position you take, you should be able to explain and justify it, and not just use terms because everyone else is using them. If you take 'learning' and 'development' to mean the same thing, you should not use both terms together, just one of them. This is like the way 'aims' and 'objectives' are often bracketed together, when many users mean both words as the same; yet just as general learning aims and specific learning objectives may be distinguished, so may learning and development.

The waters are further muddied by the use of scientific (or would-be scientific) terms to encompass all of this. Educationalists tend to speak of 'pedagogy' as the science of education, as the term for their theory of learning. The origins of this, in children's education in schools, are understandable, but when the term is used more widely, in adult education and training, it has strayed far from the original Greek definition of 'leading the child'. Keen to retain an ancient Greek term, some have suggested alternatives: Malcolm Knowles suggested andragogy, 'leading the man, or the person'; and Stewart Hase suggested heutagogy, 'leading the self', or self-directed learning. These distinctions help clarify what we are trying to accomplish in learning.

For some, all of this may be too academic. But the lesson is only to use language when it is relevant and correct; otherwise all we do is mystify and confuse, when our mission is to help and to explain.

FURTHER READING

Chapnick, S and Meloy, J (2005) From andragogy to heutagogy, Ch 3 in *Renaissance eLearning*, Wiley, San Francisco

Downs, S (1995) *Learning at Work: Effective strategies for making learning happen*, Kogan Page, London

Fee, K (2001) *A Guide to Management Development Techniques*, Kogan Page, London

L&DNA grids

03

X-REF TOOL

30 Using the learning and development cycle to plan learning interventions

Learning and development needs analysis (L&DNA) grids introduce quantitative methods to the analysis of learning and development needs. They are a means of plotting responses to specific questions on a grid and generating scores for each area under question.

One sort of grid is a self-assessment tool, where learners may be asked to score themselves against a set of criteria listed down the left-hand side of the grid, or the Y axis, choosing from a number of options along the horizontal dimension, or X axis, of the grid. The options could include 'no skill', 'need a lot of help', 'sometimes need a little help' and 'expert', and if these are then numbered from one to four the scorer has a means of building a numerical analysis of the learner's needs.

This sort of grid may also be filled in by others who know the learner, such as managers, subordinates, peers, colleagues, suppliers and customers. This leads us to another sort of grid.

A second sort of grid lists the competences required for a role down the left-hand side and arrays those who are going to score the learner along the horizontal. By counting along the line, a total score and an average score may be calculated for each competence for each learner; by counting down the line one may calculate the total score given to each learner by each scorer, and the average score each scorer gives for a competence. This is illustrated in Table 1.1.

In this simple grid, a telephonist has been scored on the basic competences of doing his or her job. Each of the scorers, numbered 1 to 5 along the top of the grid, has scored the telephonist on a scale of 1 to 5. The last two columns to the right of the grid show the telephonist's total and average

TABLE 1.1   Competence grid

Competence	1	2	3	4	5	Total	Average
Answering the telephone promptly	5	4	5	5	2	21	4.2
Giving the caller the correct greeting	4	4	4	4	2	18	3.6
Treating the caller with courtesy	3	3	3	3	1	13	2.6
Directing the call to the right person	5	4	5	4	2	20	4.0
Total	17	15	17	16	7		
Average	4.3	3.8	4.3	4.0	1.8		

score for each competence; the last two rows at the bottom of the grid show each scorer's total and average scores for the telephonist.

A brief study of these scores highlights two main findings; one is that the fifth scorer has a markedly different view of the telephonist from the other scorers; the other is that there is clearly a shared perception that the telephonist is weakest at 'treating the caller with courtesy'. The second finding gives a steer for corrective action, perhaps in the form of training, while the first shows the subjective nature of this kind of scoring.

Another sort of grid is the repertory grid. Devised by George A Kelly, this is a much more structured and formal gird, based on the theory of personal construct psychology. It contrasts two sorts of behaviour (constructs) as opposites to each competence (or) element and invites scorers to position the learner on a five- or seven-point scale between the constructs. This yields a more sophisticated profile of the learner. Repertory grids have many other applications, but this is the main way they may be applied to learning and development needs analysis.

In general, grids are useful tools for quantifying findings, and usually only cost as much staff time as is deployed to construct and administer them and analyse their findings. Additional costs may be incurred by buying software to make these tasks easier.

FURTHER READING

http://edutechwiki.unige.ch/en/Repertory_grid_technique
   (accessed November 2010)

Identifying organizational learning needs: a step-by-step approach

04

X-REF TOOL

21 Knowledge management: distinguishing data, information and knowledge

Organizational learning needs are different from individual learning needs and usually require to be addressed in different ways. The approach of the learning and development cycle remains relevant, but this step-by-step approach is an additional tool, comprising an organization-wide learning needs review that may be broken down into five distinct steps:

- *Step 1 – preparing to conduct a review.* As a first step, preparation is crucial. This should include clarifying the scope of the review, and agreeing its objectives and timetable; it should also include defining the limits of the authority of those carrying out the review, and any issues of confidentiality that may arise. Preparation is an issue not just for those conducting the review, but for those whom it will affect: thus all employees to be consulted, and anyone else who may contribute to the process, should be informed in good time of what is going to happen. This ought to include sharing the purpose and objectives of the review with all concerned.

- *Step 2 – collecting data.* The collection of data should include desk research and field research: desk research includes gathering all relevant policy statements, training plans, minutes of meetings, staff records from existing sources (eg performance reviews) and all other relevant documents; field research includes surveying employees, conducting interviews, holding focus groups and carrying out direct observation of work. Part of this step will include some initial interpretation of the data, as this may inform ongoing data collection and processing of the data into useful information.

- *Step 3 – interpreting data*. The third step involves much more detailed interpretation of the data, and its analysis. This should aim to identify not just a long list of needs, but priorities differentiated by urgency and importance (these can be plotted on a standard two-by-two matrix). Sometimes gaps and discrepancies in the data will emerge, prompting a need to revisit step 2.

- *Step 4 – developing recommendations*. Recommendations should be developed in line with the objectives set in step 1, and in consultation with those for whom the review is being undertaken – the board, senior management or other decision makers. The recommendations should be acceptable to that audience, justified with the support of reasoned arguments and evidence based on the data, costed and feasible.

- *Step 5 – preparing to implement the recommendations*. The fifth and final step is to follow up. Communicate the outcomes of the review to everyone in the organization, and work closely with senior management to ensure the recommendations are implemented. This is the step where analysis is converted to action, so cannot be taken for granted: only by completing the final step can we ensure the identified learning needs are going to be met.

This step-by-step approach may be strengthened by a good understanding, and use, of quantitative and qualitative research methods, and by an appreciation of how data may be developed into information and in turn into knowledge.

FURTHER READING

Hovland, I (2003) *Knowledge Management and Organisational Learning: An international development perspective*, Overseas Development Institute, London, http://www.odi.org.uk/resources/download/143.pdf is a valuable literature review (accessed November 2010)
http://www.training-needs-analysis.co.uk/index.php?option=com_content &view=article&id=51&Itemid=66 has an alternative, seven-step plan (accessed November 2010)

Performance analysis quadrant

05

X-REF TOOLS

3 L&DNA grids
4 Identifying organizational learning needs: a step-by-step approach

---

Learning and development interventions are just one means of solving performance problems. The performance analysis quadrant (PAQ) is a tool to help identify where learning and development can help.

When collecting and processing data and information, when analysing individual, team and organizational needs, the investigating manager has to determine what sort of intervention will provide the best solution to meet the needs. The considerations here may be reduced to questions about whether the subject (individual, team or organization) has the knowledge, skills and competence to fulfil its remit, and whether the subject has the right attitude or culture.

The range of possible solutions may be classified into four sets, which make up the four parts of the PAQ: learning and development; recruitment and selection; motivation; and resources or environment.

These four sets are arrayed in the PAQ by constructing two axes around the questions about knowledge, skills and competence – or capability – and attitude or culture. Capability forms the vertical axis, from low capability at the foot to high capability at the top, and attitude the horizontal axis, from poor attitude on the left to good attitude on the right, yielding the quadrant in Figure 1.1.

Taking the example of an individual's needs analysed using the PAQ, if the person has the knowledge and skills needed to do a job well, but is underperforming, this implies that the problem is motivational, that the individual does not have sufficient desire or incentive to meet the performance requirement. This is manifested as a poor attitude combined with high capability, placing the individual in the top left-hand quarter. Learning

FIGURE 1.1   Performance analysis quadrant

	MOTIVATION	RESOURCES/ENVIRONMENT
Capability	RECRUITMENT & SELECTION	LEARNING & DEVELOPMENT

Attitude

and development cannot help in this case, unless their purpose is purely motivational.

If the individual has both low capability and poor attitude, placing him or her in the bottom left quarter, then that implies a recruitment or selection problem. If the individual is in the wrong job, then no amount of learning and development is likely to help.

In the converse case, if the individual has both a good attitude and high capability, then the implication is that lack of sufficient or appropriate resources, including the possibility of poor management or deficiencies in the working environment, lies at the root of the problem. This is represented in the top right-hand quarter, and once again learning and development are unlikely to provide the solution, or at least not the sole solution.

Only in the case of an individual with a good attitude but low capability, represented by the bottom right-hand quarter, is a learning and development intervention likely to be the key solution.

Debates will continue about the circumstances in which learning and development may help, and some of us will take a more generous interpretation, but the lesson of the PAQ is that resources for learning and development are likely to have the most impact, and the highest success rates, where they address the sort of problems in the bottom right-hand quarter, where a learning and development solution is essential.

FURTHER READING

http://www.nwlink.com/~donclark/hrd/isd/analyze_system.html (accessed November 2010)

The learning curve

X-REF TOOLS

2   Understanding learning, development, education and training

8   Informal and non-formal learning

The learning curve is a bit of a cliché, frequently used and misused. People talk about any new learning experience, especially a challenging one, as a learning curve, but this is a loose, colloquial use of the term, and a distortion of its true meaning. Properly used and understood, it is an invaluable tool for learning and development professionals.

The learning curve is an S curve on a graph, as shown in Figure 1.2. It may be thought of as a journey, where the traveller progresses along, steadily, on a straight road; then the road turns uphill and the journey becomes harder work, before the road levels off again at the top of the hill, and the traveller is making steady progress again, but at a higher level.

I do not wish to labour the metaphor, but it can be applied to a work situation. Employees may be working away steadily until they encounter

FIGURE 1.2   The learning curve

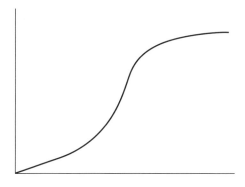

something new, whereupon they struggle a bit until they learn how to tackle this new development, and then they continue to work away, but now perhaps more productively, or to a higher standard, as a result of the learning.

But this is an example of the classic misuse, which is to talk about a steep or sharp learning curve when what is meant is that the learning is difficult; the metaphor of the uphill journey encourages this misunderstanding. In fact, if the curve is steep, this means the learning is quick and easy; a slow ascent of a gentler curve would indicate a more challenging learning experience.

Perhaps we should conceive a new metaphor, but the best I can suggest is to reverse the gravity, so that the steep curve goes downwards like a slide, working in the learner's favour. I'm sure there must be a better way of representing the curve to correct the misuse and render greater clarity to its undoubted relevance.

When applying the curve to employee development, it helps to understand what the employee is experiencing as a learner. Often experienced operators, or experts, cannot understand how a novice finds difficult that which they regard as straightforward. The curve helps explain this. Comparative analysis of the learning curves for acquiring different skills or job competences can help inform job design, learning interventions, reward structures, talent management plans and more.

Illustrative example

A new teacher or trainer will take much longer to prepare a lesson plan for a learning intervention than a more experienced teacher or trainer. Any combination of a new role, new subject material and a new audience – even if the novice is very confident about one or more of these components – will render the task of preparation much more difficult and time-consuming than it is for someone more experienced. The experience of repeating this task for different subjects and different audiences will move novices along the learning curve until they reach the plateau at the top of the curve and become more accomplished in the role.

FURTHER READING

Dar-El, Ezey M (2011) *Human Learning: From learning curves to learning organisations*, Springer, New York

http://www.managementaccountant.in/2007/04/learning-curve-theory.html (accessed November 2010)

Bloom's taxonomy of learning domains

X-REF TOOLS

Benjamin Bloom developed his taxonomy of learning domains in 1956, and although his target audience was educationalists and academics it has great significance for all kinds of learning. It is useful as a theoretical tool that helps us to understand how people learn and can help shape learning objectives.

There are three broad domains in Bloom's taxonomy:

- affective;
- psychomotor; and
- cognitive.

The affective domain is about how the learner reacts emotionally, and so affective objectives are about attitudes and feelings. Bloom divided them into five levels (from lowest to highest): receiving, responding, valuing, organizing and characterizing.

Illustrative example

The learner listens to a story about someone losing his or her job (receiving); the learner asks questions to establish why this happened (responding); the learner considers how the unemployed person feels (valuing); the learner compares this with stories or his or her experience of other people losing their job (organizing); and the learner decides whether it was a good or bad thing that the person lost the job (characterizing).

The psychomotor domain is about acquiring manual skills. Bloom did not subdivide this domain, though others have subsequently attempted it. One version, by R H Dave, subdivides the domain into imitation, manipulation, precision, articulation and naturalization.

Illustrative example

The learner copies other actions (imitation); the learner re-creates the actions from memory (manipulation); the learner repeatedly and reliably practises the actions (precision); the learner adapts the skill to another context (articulation); and the learner achieves mastery of the skill in all contexts (naturalization).

The psychomotor domain is likely to be of interest to many trainers, and offers an alternative to the progressive model of unconscious incompetence (I don't know what I can't do), to conscious incompetence (I still can't do it, but I know what it is I can't do), to conscious competence (I can now do it, but I have to think about it), to unconscious competence (I can do it almost without thinking). This has a bearing on how we practise skills.

The cognitive domain is about acquiring more cerebral knowledge. Bloom divided it into six levels (from lowest to highest): knowledge, comprehension, application, analysis, synthesis and evaluation.

The learner learns facts, figures and basic ideas (knowledge); the learner interprets these facts, figures or ideas (comprehension); the learner uses the knowledge in a new context (application); the learner breaks down the knowledge into its constituent parts and considers its interrelationships (analysis); the learner combines the knowledge, applications and analysis to produce something new (synthesis); and the learner draws conclusions and makes judgements (evaluation).

Taken together, the taxonomy amounts to a range of types of learning objective, which may be interpreted to parallel the three dimensions of learning: attitudes, skills and knowledge. Whether they form the exact hierarchy advocated by Bloom is controversial, but essentially irrelevant to any practical application of the tool.

Bloom's taxonomy has many practical applications. It can be used to review how learning activities may contribute to learning objectives. It can help decide whether the activities that make up a learning intervention are working in harmony. It can be used to choose appropriate learner objectives to meet identified needs. And it can provide insight into how people learn. All of this may contribute to the analysis of learning and development needs, and to the planning of learning interventions.

FURTHER READING

Anderson, L W and Krathwohl, D R (eds) (2001) *A Taxonomy for Learning, Teaching, and Assessing: A revision of Bloom's taxonomy of educational objectives*, Allyn & Bacon, Boston, MA

Bloom, B S (1956) *Taxonomy of Educational Objectives: The classification of educational goals*, Susan Fauer, Chicago

Marzano, R and Kendall J, (2007) *The New Taxonomy of Educational Objectives*, Corwin Press, Thousand Oaks, CA

08 Informal and non-formal learning

X-REF TOOLS

2 Understanding learning, development, education and training

6 The learning curve

33 Using different approaches to learning and development

Informal learning is usually assumed to mean learning that takes place inadvertently, even subconsciously, and is rarely planned. Non-formal learning is usually considered to be planned learning that takes place away from the classroom, and does not follow an accredited programme or lead to a qualification.

However, these definitions are set from the perspective of educationalists, who see only classroom-based and certificated learning as 'formal'. I beg to differ.

I would contend that any planned learning intervention, especially any that is subjected to summative assessment and confers some sort of award, ought to be regarded as formal. I certainly see the more organized expressions of work-based learning in this category.

Many private sector training providers and voluntary organizations offer competence-based qualification programmes, such as, in the UK, National Vocational Qualifications, involving assessment of evidence generated from work experience, with tutorial support mainly at a distance, and just occasional face-to-face tutorial events as milestones. Barely a whiff of the classroom, no educational institution and no exams, but this is still formal learning.

However, many loose work-based learning initiatives (such as 'sitting-by-Nellie'), innovative organized learning experiences such as those using the outdoor environment, and even some of the more casual classroom-based events clearly fall within the category of non-formal learning.

The layperson might argue that the terms 'informal' and 'non-formal' essentially mean the same thing, but in the context of learning they offer a valid distinction, and clearly differentiate two sorts of learning from the more widely recognized formal learning. Thus they offer a valuable tool for distinguishing different approaches, and understanding their potential and their limitations.

Thinking about formal, non-formal and informal learning encourages us to think about what goes on in the learning process. There are various theories about how we use our brain to learn, including the theory of left versus right brain, and the use of the whole brain.

Some of this thinking originated from the research in the 1960s of the Nobel Prize-winner Roger W Sperry. He discovered that the human brain has two very different ways of thinking. One, the right brain way, is visual and processes information in an intuitive and simultaneous way, looking first at the whole picture and then the details. The other, the left brain way, is verbal and processes information in an analytical and sequential way, looking first at the pieces and then putting them together to get the whole.

Advocates of the left versus right brain theory argue that each of us shows a preference for one kind of thinking over the other. On the other hand, many scientists are sceptical of the theory, but it remains a useful theory for illustrating different ways of seeing things and different ways of learning, especially in the arena of informal and non-formal learning.

FURTHER READING

Colley, H, Hodkinson, P and Malcolm, J (2002) *Non-Formal Learning: Mapping the conceptual terrain: a consultation report*, Leeds: University of Leeds Lifelong Learning Institute, 2002. Also available in the Informal Education Archives: http://www.infed.org/archives/e-texts/colley_informal_learning.htm (accessed November 2010)

http://www.funderstanding.com/content/right-brain-vs-left-brain (accessed November 2010)

http://www.rense.com/general2/rb.htm offers a sceptical view of the left versus right brain theory (accessed November 2010)

http://www.testcafe.com/lbrb/ has a test that shows whether your preference is for the left or the right side of the brain (accessed November 2010)

09 Kolb's experiential learning cycle

X-REF TOOLS

10 Honey and Mumford's learning styles
55 How to organize work-based learning
56 Guided practice
68 Simulation

Perhaps one of the most common and best-known learning tools is David Kolb's experiential learning cycle, first developed in association with Roger Fry in the 1970s.

Experiential learning or, crudely, learning by doing is a cornerstone of successful learning and development. It is the essence of work-based learning, for example, and may be traced as far back as the old saw attributed to Confucius: 'Tell me and I forget; show me and I remember; involve me and I understand.' Kolb's cycle, or circle, is founded in this precept, but is a little more sophisticated and, to some, controversial, as it appears to argue that human behaviour – and learning – follows rigid patterns. However, most people recognize enough in the cycle to find it a useful tool when designing learning interventions and trying to make the most of hands-on experience.

Kolb's experiential learning cycle describes four phases that follow each other in sequence, namely:

- *experience* – the learner's immediate or concrete experiences;
- *reflection* – also known as observations and reflections, which the learner derives from his or her concrete experience;
- *conceptualization* – also known as abstract conceptualization, when the learner's reflections are generalized;
- *experimentation* – or active experimentation, when ideas are tested, and related and applied to new experiences.

The learner may begin by having a concrete experience, then reflect upon it, then generalize from the experience and reflections, forming an abstract concept, and then apply that concept, testing it in new experience (although Kolb, in fact, argues that the learner may start at any point in the cycle). This approach breaks down what's involved in learning a new work skill, or part of a job, and thus helps facilitate learning for work. The cycle is shown in Figure 1.3.

FIGURE 1.3 Kolb's experiential learning cycle

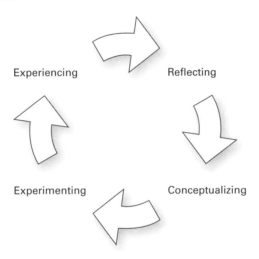

Experiencing

Reflecting

Experimenting

Conceptualizing

Kolb argues that understanding how people learn, which is what the cycle is about, lies at the heart of devising and implementing successful learning and development, and accomplishing our goals.

Illustrative example

A new user of word processing software, trying it out without any prior instruction, learns by doing, by experiencing the creation of a document, and quickly learns how to format text by highlighting sections and clicking buttons to make it bold, italic or underlined. When reflecting on how this works, the user is not just committing these processes to memory, but is starting to think about what else may be possible. The user forms a general concept that highlighting text opens it to all sorts of other kinds of formatting, and then tests this concept by experimenting with new formats, such as upper case or strikethrough. The user continues to experience new possibilities in the software, and continues on the cycle of experiential learning.

FURTHER READING

Kolb, D A (1983) *Experiential Learning: Experience as the source of learning and development*, FT Prentice Hall, Harlow

Pickles, T and Greenaway, R (nd) Experiential learning articles and critiques of David Kolb's theory, http://reviewing.co.uk/research/experiential.learning.htm (accessed November 2010)

Smith, M K (2001) David A. Kolb on experiential learning, *Encyclopedia of Informal Education*, http://www.infed.org/biblio/b-explrn.htm (accessed November 2010)

Honey and Mumford's learning styles

X-REF TOOLS

9   Kolb's experiential learning cycle
11 Rose's learning styles
27 Learning methods and styles grid

David Kolb has spent many years developing the original work of his experiential learning cycle and expanding it to adjacent ideas, such as an inventory of learning styles. Many competing classifications of learning styles have developed, and perhaps foremost among these is that of Peter Honey and Alan Mumford, derived from Kolb's cycle, and first published in 1982.

Honey and Mumford take each of the four phases of Kolb's cycle and identify each with a particular learning style. They go on to argue that every learner has a preference for one style or another.

The four styles relate to each of the four phase of Kolb's cycle as follows:

- experiencing – activist;
- reflecting – reflector;
- conceptualizing – theorist;
- experimenting – pragmatist.

The learner who prefers to act – doing things and accumulating concrete experience – is characterized as an activist. The learner who likes to spend time reviewing his or her experience and reflecting upon problems is characterized as a reflector. The learner who takes a more cerebral approach, the opposite of the activist, and focuses on understanding concepts is a theorist. And the learner who likes to plan, explore options and test theories is a pragmatist.

Of course, it is too facile to categorize every learner as merely one of four set types. None of us fits neatly into convenient pigeonholes like this. But these are useful indicators of a predominant preference for each learner, even·if many individual examples are hybrids, and they are valuable reference points in constructing learning interventions. In order to be effective, general learning and development approaches need to accommodate the preferred learning styles of all four types, or risk failing the learners whose preferred styles are not included.

All good so far, and it seems common sense that people learn in different ways, but the Honey and Mumford classification and indeed all learning styles classifications have been criticized by psychologists and neuroscientists as having no scientifically proven basis, lacking evidential support and contradicting studies showing that our senses work in unison and don't lend themselves to this sort of differentiation. As the controversy continues, Honey and Mumford's learning styles model continues to be very popular.

FURTHER READING

Honey, P and Mumford, A (1982) *Manual of Learning Styles*, Peter Honey Publications, Maidenhead
http://www.campaign-for-learning.org.uk/cfl/yourlearning/whatlearner.asp (accessed November 2010)

Rose's learning styles

11

In contrast to Honey and Mumford's model, the other popular learning styles model is simple and intuitive, being based on how we perceive things through our biological senses. It is derived from Colin Rose's work on accelerated learning, is closely related to the ideas of neuro-linguistic programming (NLP), and traces its roots back to early-20th-century ideas about the education of children, such as the Montessori method. This model distinguishes three main learning styles: visual, auditory, and kinaesthetic or tactile.

- *visual:* looking at things – watching and reading;
- *auditory:* not just listening, but speaking as well;
- *kinaesthetic/tactile:* doing things, and using the sense of touch.

Learners who prefer the visual style learn best, according to this model, when they can look at things, including pictures and diagrams, use visual cues, watch videos and live demonstrations, and take in information primarily through their eyes. This corresponds with the theory that most communication, even verbal communication, is conducted primarily through body language and facial expressions.

Learners who prefer the auditory style learn best, according to this model, when they can get into conversation with their tutor, mentor or other learners, when they can use speech and language, and when they can listen to lectures or audio recordings.

Learners who prefer the tactile/kinaesthetic style learn best, according to this model, when they can touch things and get their hands on to raw materials, tools and equipment. There is a clear correlation between this style, and the activist style in Honey and Mumford's model, where the learner prefers learning by doing.

Illustrative example

When people try to spell a word, if they try to 'see' the word in their 'mind's eye', this suggests they have a preference for the visual style; if they try to sound the word phonetically, this suggests a preference for the auditory style; and if they try writing out the word until it 'feels' right, this suggests a preference for the tactile style. When reading fiction, someone with a visual style preference should enjoy descriptive imagery, someone with an auditory style preference should enjoy dialogue, as it conveys a sense of the characters talking, and someone with a tactile style preference should prefer a swift-moving plot, perhaps with plenty of action.

Perhaps the attraction of Rose's model is that it is so simple, representing little more than a claim that we all prefer to draw upon one of our senses, which is dominant. Interestingly, the model downgrades the senses of taste and smell, and while this may be understandable for many occupational applications of learning it will certainly not be the case in the realm of cooking, catering, and food and drink tasting, among other occupations where taste and smell are paramount. Regardless of how simple it may be, this remains a useful tool when thinking about how people learn and how we can best help them.

FURTHER READING

Riding, R and Rayner, S (1998) *Cognitive Styles and Learning Strategies: Understanding style differences in learning and behaviour*, David Fulton, London

Rose, C and Meyer, A (eds) (2006) *Learning Styles: A practical reader in the universal design for learning*, Harvard Education Press, Cambridge, MA

http://www.chaminade.org/inspire/learnstl.htm

Overcoming barriers to learning

X-REF TOOLS

14 How to develop a learning culture

15 How to develop a learning organization

Barriers to learning come in many forms. The key to overcoming them is first to recognize the main types of barrier and secondly to have strategies available to address and overcome them. Table 1.2 summarizes the main barriers and how to deal with them.

TABLE 1.2 Barriers to learning

The barriers	The solutions
Barriers to entering learning, or to pursuing and completing the learning process, such as bureaucratic procedures for entering learning and/or completing learning.	Simplify. Reduce red tape, ie any unnecessary paperwork. Open access to opportunities to as many people as possible. Have clear signposting and make sure progression routes are clear.
Organizational/cultural barriers in the form of resistance to learning and development initiatives. This may be because of differences between management's learning model and that of the learners, or it could be caused by deeper rifts in the organization, perhaps around employee relations issues.	Build a shared understanding of the place of learning in the organization, how it contributes to goals, and how it benefits everyone. Recognize where the points of resistance lie and find ways to counter them – directly and indirectly.

TABLE 1.2   *Continued*

The barriers	The solutions
Lack of motivation from learners, including not just an unwillingness to learn but, perhaps more deeply seated, a lack of belief in their ability to learn.	At the organizational level, develop a learning culture. At the individual level, encourage learners and prospective learners whenever possible, and offer easy first steps to get them engaged. Be positive. Reward success in learning.
The stigma of learning, including learners' fears of exposing their weaknesses or failings, especially to their colleagues, subordinates and bosses.	Learning needs to be seen as a positive process and as a means to an end – the way to succeed in the organization. There also needs to be a culture of openness and one where people feel empowered to make mistakes and get things wrong – as long as they learn from them.
Time barriers, including lack of sufficient time to undertake the learning, or bad timing in scheduling learning opportunities.	Ask what works best. Evaluate. Learn from mistakes. Aim to schedule for times that suit the learners best, and always to allow plenty of time for learning.
Unattractive learning opportunities, including use of inconvenient or inappropriate locations, the learning being unfit for purpose or not suited to the prevailing learning style preferences, or inappropriate learning methods or group composition.	The counter to this is good practice in designing and organizing learning. Use the tools in this book. Assess how well they work. Adapt accordingly. Always take account of feedback from learners and from others involved in learning.
Costs and lack of facilities or resources.	Control costs, and avoid waste, but also fight for budgets. Attract the best possible resources for learning, and apply them efficiently and effectively.

TABLE 1.2   *Continued*

The barriers	The solutions
Discriminatory barriers – whether attitudinal, organizational or practical – that exclude learners with different abilities or different work patterns from engaging with other learners or the learning process.	Consider the different needs of different abilities of learners. If in doubt, seek them out and ask them. And take into account the organization's working practices.
How easy the learning is to access and understand (whether the level of the learning is appropriate).	This requires constant testing of processes for matching the individual learner's needs to the right learning opportunities. Evaluation tools should pick up evidence of some learners struggling with things that others find easy.
Whether learning offers are relevant to learners' needs and are understood by learners as such.	Listen to learners. Use learning needs analysis tools that work. Market learning opportunities effectively, with the emphasis on what's in it for the learner.

FURTHER READING

Dawson, C (2005) *Returning to Learning: A practical handbook for adults returning to education*, How To Books, Oxford

Hoult, E (2006) *Learning Support for Mature Students*, Sage Publications, London

http://honolulu.hawaii.edu/intranet/committees/FacDevCom/guidebk/teachtip/adults-2.htm (accessed December 2010)

http://www.skillsdevelopment.org/pdf/Addressing%20Barriers%20to%20Learning%20Briefing%20Notes.pdf (accessed December 2010)

http://www.tjtaylor.net/research/The-Seven-E-Learning-Barriers-facing-Employees-Penina-Mungania-2003.pdf (accessed December 2010)

13 Johari window

X-REF TOOLS

10 Honey and Mumford's learning styles

11 Rose's learning styles

32 Personal development planning

This tool takes its name, unusually, from an amalgam of the first names of Joseph Luft and Harry Ingham, who devised it in the 1960s (some date its origins as far back as 1955) to help people better understand their communication and relationships with others.

The Johari window is essentially a self-assessment tool, and may be understood as a window into the self. Charles Handy uses a slightly different metaphor, when he calls it the Johari house, and identifies each of the four quadrants as a room in the house.

The Johari window is a two-by-two matrix, in which the subject is the learner, or the self, and the two dimensions are what is known, or not known, about the self by others (on the vertical axis), and what is known, or not known, about the self by one's self (on the horizontal axis). The matrix is shown in Figure 1.4.

The arena, or open, quadrant represents what is known about the self to one's self as well as others. These are the subject's most visible characteristics.

The hidden, or façade, quadrant represents what is known about the self to one's self but not to others. These are the subject's least visible characteristics.

The blind spot quadrant represents what is known about the self to others but not to one's self. These are the subject's characteristics that are apparent to others but have somehow been missed by the subject.

The unknown quadrant represents what is known about the self neither by one's self nor by others. This represents an area for new development.

The standard analysis, using the Johari window, is conducted by asking the subject, and others who know the subject, to place each of the following

FIGURE 1.4   Johari window

	Known to self	Not known to self
Known to others	**ARENA**	**BLIND SPOT**
Not known to others	**HIDDEN**	**UNKNOWN**

56 adjectives describing the subject into one of the four quadrants: able, accepting, adaptable, bold, brave, calm, caring, cheerful, clever, complex, confident, dependable, dignified, energetic, extroverted, friendly, giving, happy, helpful, idealistic, independent, ingenious, intelligent, introverted, kind, knowledgeable, logical, loving, mature, modest, nervous, observant, organized, patient, powerful, proud, quiet, reflective, relaxed, religious, responsive, searching, self-assertive, self-conscious, sensible, sentimental, shy, silly, smart, spontaneous, sympathetic, tense, trustworthy, warm, wise and witty.

This then builds up a picture of how much of each person's characteristics is open, hidden, unknown or part of the person's blind spot. Subsequent discussion or further analysis should focus on developing the open area, as this improves team working and organizational cohesion. Learning and development interventions may form an important part of this process, by encouraging the learner to open up about him- or herself, thus moving information from the hidden area to the open area, and by encouraging others to help reveal the blind spot to the learner. The unknown area will require experimentation with new and perhaps challenging behaviours.

The Johari window enables a manager to understand learners better and thence develop learning and development solutions that better address their individual needs.

FURTHER READING

Luft, J and Ingham, H (1961) The Johari window: a graphic model of interpersonal awareness, *Human Relations Training News*, http://www.convivendo.net/wp-content/uploads/2009/05/johari-window-articolo-originale1.pdf (accessed November 2010)
http://kevan.org/johari, an interactive online version (accessed November 2010)

14 How to develop a learning culture

Culture is a much misunderstood concept, but essentially it is the antonym of nature: anything that does not occur in nature without the intervention of humankind, and any human development that is not simply about our genetics, falls within the realm of culture. A specific culture is about having a shared set of attitudes, values, goals and practices.

A learning culture, like any sort of culture, is defined qualitatively, and is hard to pin down in quantitative terms, but it is broadly recognized as a climate within an organization where people enjoy learning and see it as one of the benefits of working there, where people welcome and seek out opportunities to learn, and where work is often arranged to build in learning experiences. In other words, it is where the people of an organization share a positive set of attitudes, values, goals and practices around learning.

It is possible to identify distinguishing characteristics to help us recognize where a learning culture exists. Peter Senge is the organizational development theorist who has had most to say about this. He has identified five dimensions of a learning culture – personal mastery; mental models; shared vision; team learning; and system thinking – as summarized in Table 1.3.

TABLE 1.3   Senge's dimensions of a learning culture

Dimension	Description
Personal mastery	Creating an environment that encourages the development of personal and organizational goals in partnership with others.
Mental models	Using visualization or 'internal pictures' to help shape behaviour and decisions.
Shared vision	Winning group commitment by developing shared images of how the future should look.
Team learning	Encouraging collective thinking and working, so that a group's capacity to develop intelligence and ability is greater than the sum of its individual members' talents.
System thinking	Developing the ability to see the 'big picture' within an organization, and understanding how changes in one part affect the whole system.

The challenge for organizations, and the purpose of this tool, is to convert these theoretical precepts into practical guidance specific to each organization, to find ways to inculcate a learning culture. The application of Senge's five dimensions is one useful starting point.

FURTHER READING

Conner, M and Clawson, J (2004) *Creating a Learning Culture: Strategy, technology, and practice*, Cambridge University Press, Cambridge
Saylor, J (2009) *Developing a Learning Culture*, www.lulu.com
Senge, P (1990) *The Fifth Discipline: The art and practice of the learning organization*, Doubleday, New York
http://www.cipd.co.uk/helpingpeoplelearn/_lrncltre.htm, a collection of case studies (accessed November 2010)

15 How to develop a learning organization

X-REF TOOLS

12 Overcoming barriers to learning

14 How to develop a learning culture

16 The learning value chain

21 Knowledge management: distinguishing data, information and knowledge

22 The five aspects of talent management

A 'learning organization' is an ill-defined concept, but a popular one. It is a term for any organization that promotes and celebrates learning, where individuals have plenty of opportunities to learn and develop, and where everyone in the organization collectively develops in the realization of the organization's goals.

The concept of the learning organization relates closely to several other strategic tools in this book. Managing the knowledge within an organization is part of building a learning organization; the learning organization is a vehicle for accomplishing effective talent management; and it is the organizational expression of a learning culture.

Peter Senge (1990) defines a learning organization as one 'where people continually expand their capacity to create the results they truly desire, where new and expansive patterns of thinking are nurtured, where collective aspiration is set free, and where people are continually learning to see the whole together'. This implies individuals having a great degree of control over what they do, and being encouraged to experiment, explore and above all learn.

Pedler, Burgoyne and Boydell (1991) offer this definition: 'A learning organisation is an organisation which facilitates the learning of all its members and constantly transforms itself.' They also identify five characteristics of a learning organization: strategy; structures; learning opportunities; looking in; and looking out. These characteristics give us a guide to action, a guide for how to develop a learning organization:

- *Strategy.* The organization needs to ensure that it has a learning approach to strategy and policy development, encouraging the broadest possible participation in research, strategy setting and development.

- *Structures.* The organization's structures need to be enabling – to afford opportunities for learning, movement, changes in roles, etc. The organization should probably have a flatter, less hierarchical structure, certainly a flexible one.

- *Learning opportunities.* The organization should offer plenty of learning and development opportunities for everyone. More than that, it should foster a climate where questioning, reflection, experimenting and freedom to make mistakes are all encouraged.

- *Looking in.* The importance of this introspection is that all parts of the organization need to communicate and collaborate, to ensure an interchange of ideas and experiences. The way the organization offers incentives and other rewards needs to reflect this.

- *Looking out.* Outward-facing staff need to gather information about the external world, including customers, suppliers and competitors, and feed it back into the organization, and external networks need to be developed to draw on good practice elsewhere.

The benefits of all of this should be seen in enhanced organizational metrics, such as increased staff satisfaction and reduced staff turnover. The benefits should also be seen in improved performance and in better quality, higher income and increased profits (where applicable). The learning organization is just a better organization all round.

FURTHER READING

Clarke, A (2001) *Learning Organisations*, National Institute of Adult Continuing Education, Leicester

Pedler, M, Burgoyne, J and Boydell, T (1991) *The Learning Company*, McGraw-Hill, London

Senge, P (1990) *The Fifth Discipline: The art and practice of the learning organization*, Doubleday, New York

16 The learning value chain

X-REF TOOLS

- **2** Understanding learning, development, education and training
- **6** The learning curve
- **7** Bloom's taxonomy of learning domains
- **9** Kolb's experiential learning cycle
- **40** Learning design: the five dimensions
- **56** Guided practice

Many people view learning as being solely, or at least mainly, about knowledge transfer, from a teacher or trainer, or perhaps a textbook, to the learner. This is a common fault in e-learning, for example, where this oversimplistic view of learning is often encountered. In fact, learning is much more complex: yes, we learn when we passively read something, or watch a video, or listen to a lecturer. But we learn more when we get active, and this is especially true of learning for work, where the idea is to apply our learning, practise our skills and develop new competences.

To assist with this, the learning value chain is a tool I have developed, drawing on the work of David Kolb with his experiential learning cycle (1983) (see tool 9) and Michael Porter with his value chain (1985). Compare it also with Roberto Moretti's five processes of practice (2009) (see tool 56). The new tool identifies five distinct learning processes:

1 *knowledge acquisition*, when learners acquire information and convert it to knowledge;

2 *reflection*, when learners apply knowledge to their work situation and reflect on its impact;

3 *practice*, when learners practise new skills or behaviours, either at work or in a simulated environment;

4 *interaction*, when learners exchange experiences with other learners and synthesize new experience;

5 *escalation*, when learners build on their newly acquired skills and behaviours to develop new knowledge, apply it and develop new skills and behaviours.

In the learning value chain diagram, Figure 1.5, these five processes occur in a sequence, each building on the value of the preceding process. It is not essential that these processes occur in this order, but taken together like this they add the most value. The diagram is completed by sample support inputs identified for each process, as a means to better understand what each process is about, by underpinning people management and development inputs, and formal and non-formal education and training inputs.

FIGURE 1.5   The learning value chain

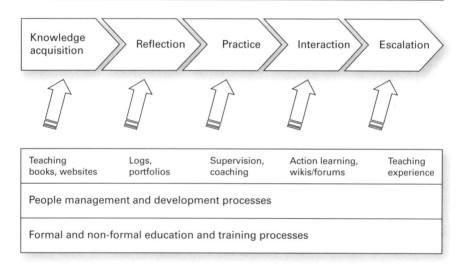

Knowledge acquisition	Reflection	Practice	Interaction	Escalation

Teaching books, websites	Logs, portfolios	Supervision, coaching	Action learning, wikis/forums	Teaching experience

People management and development processes

Formal and non-formal education and training processes

The learning value chain illustrates that learning is a complex sum of processes, not just about the acquisition of information by learners, but about the consideration and testing of that information, the exchange of more information with others, and the application of the new knowledge and skills to new situations where they are once again questioned. Indeed, learning can take place without the initial supply of information; this supply can be a vital catalyst, and is rightly recognized as very important, but it is not essential, and it is not the pre-eminent process.

FURTHER READING

This tool was originally developed by the author as a contribution to consultancy work for a corporate client, and was first recorded in his blog on 28 October 2009, at http://learnforeverblog.blogspot.com.

Kolb, D A (1983) *Experiential Learning: Experience as the source of learning and development*, FT Prentice Hall, Harlow

Moretti, R (2009) *Practice Made Perfect*

Porter, M (1985) *Competitive Advantage*, Free Press, New York

Accelerated learning

17

X-REF TOOLS

11 Rose's learning styles

19 Gardner's multiple intelligences

21 Knowledge management: distinguishing data, information and knowledge

Accelerated learning is a tool, or system, that claims to help people learn faster and more effectively. It is based on the principle of matching learning techniques to individuals' learning style preferences, and derives largely from Colin Rose's work on learning styles, which in some applications are developed further than the three basic styles we saw in tool 11.

But it goes further. Accelerated learning also draws on some of the shared wisdom about learning that underpins many of the other tools in this book – a holistic approach, the principle of being learner centred, activity as opposed to passivity in learning, and learning as creation of knowledge rather than consumption of information. Accelerated learning is also closely related to the work of Georgi Lozanov on 'suggestopedia' and accelerated language learning.

This tool is not just about speeding up learning; it is about clarity in objective setting and reviewing, getting the learning environment right, making the most of memory techniques such as mnemonics and mind mapping, breaking down learning into smaller and more digestible parts, and added stimuli such as listening to music while reading. The point of all of this is to embed learning better, so that knowledge is retained and built upon, and to encourage people to improve their learning habits.

With such a range of concepts involved, the accelerated learning movement has become rather diverse, with various diverging and competing theories around. What they retain in common is a perspective of getting the brain ready to learn, and thus enabling learners to learn faster and better.

The term may be a misnomer, in that it tends to imply 'speed learning', when how quick the learning is may not be the most important benefit. In the context of learning for work, the most important benefit may be that it makes transfer of learning to the work application more effective.

Advocates of accelerated learning can be intense and evangelical, and this can be off-putting, but their passion derives from some solid founding principles that may be seen in other tools as well. Understanding accelerated learning can help with a general understanding of what makes learning effective, and with placing appropriate emphasis on good learning practice.

FURTHER READING

Best, B (2006) *Accelerated Learning Pocketbook*, Management Pocketbooks, Alresford

Meier, D (2000) *The Accelerated Learning Handbook: A creative guide to designing and delivering faster, more effective training programs*, McGraw-Hill, New York

Rose, C (1985) *Accelerated Learning*, Accelerated Learning Systems, Aylesbury

http://www.acceleratedlearning.com

http://www.jwelford.demon.co.uk/brainwaremap/suggest.html

Emotional intelligence

18

> **X-REF TOOLS**
>
> **8** Informal and non-formal learning
>
> **19** Gardner's multiple intelligences
>
> **20** Neuro-linguistic programming

Daniel Goleman may not have discovered the term 'emotional intelligence' or invented the concept, but the model he promulgated in 1995 did more than anything beforehand to bring the idea to mass attention and influence learning and development, among other things. At its heart is the notion that too much emphasis has been placed on intellectual intelligence and that we need to shift the balance more to what our emotions tell us: that we need to think less of our IQ and more of our EQ.

This chimes with popular thinking about the use of the right brain versus the left brain, and with the idea of a more sensitive, typically feminine perspective as distinct from a more logical, typically masculine perspective. It is a call to arms to tune into our feelings and those of others.

Emotional intelligence is both a concept for life and work and a more specific behavioural model for how we conduct ourselves in order to be more effective and to better understand the world around us, including our business organization and its stakeholders. Goleman argued that we should understand ourselves, and our own goals, intentions and responses, as well as understanding others and their feelings.

Goleman identified five domains of emotional intelligence as:

- knowing one's emotions;
- managing one's own emotions;
- motivating oneself;
- recognizing and understanding other people's emotions; and
- managing relationships, or managing the emotions of others.

Building on this, Goleman developed a range of resources to support this and to help people implement his ideas, such as his emotional competence framework. Others have developed further resources, such as Cary Cherniss's 19 practical examples of how emotional intelligence contributes to the bottom line. These resources pay tribute to the idea that we can change our emotional behaviour.

A popular misconception is to regard the way we feel as being an unchangeable aspect of our individual personalities. Goleman and his followers see our emotional intelligence as something we can work on and as a set of capabilities we can improve. A common thread in the literature is moving through a series of phases of greater and greater understanding: from initial self-awareness of how one behaves, understanding one's emotions and reactions, to learning how to manage those emotions, including using techniques to master potentially destructive feelings like anxiety, to awareness of others' emotions and learning how to manage relationships accordingly.

Those who have used emotional intelligence as a tool report that they improve their decision making by learning when and why to trust their 'gut feelings', and that they work better with others, by understanding not just what other people are saying, but why. Clearly there are lessons here for us all to learn.

FURTHER READING

Chapman, M (2001) *The Emotional Intelligence Pocketbook*, Management Pocketbooks, Alresford

Cherniss, C (1999) The business case for emotional intelligence, http://www.eiconsortium.org/reports/business_case_for_ei.html (accessed December 2010)

Goleman, D (1995) *Emotional Intelligence: Why it can matter more than IQ*, Bloomsbury, London

Goleman, D (1999) *Working with Emotional Intelligence*, Bloomsbury, London

Stein, S (2009) *Emotional Intelligence for Dummies*, Wiley, Mississauga, ON

http://www.eiconsortium.org/

http://www.unh.edu/emotional_intelligence/

Gardner's multiple intelligences

Howard Gardner developed his theory of multiple intelligences in 1993, and expounded seven: linguistic, logic-mathematical, musical, spatial, bodily kinaesthetic, interpersonal and intrapersonal. In 1999, he added an eighth, naturalist intelligence, and at the time of writing he is considering a ninth, existential or moral intelligence.

Gardner's starting point was that traditional theories of intelligence, with their emphasis on the intelligence quotient, or IQ, were inadequate in recognizing and understanding the many ways in which people think, learn and develop. Like the theory of emotional intelligence, perhaps even more so, Gardner's theory is hotly disputed in academic circles, but its practical value is widely acknowledged, albeit with some claiming this is just common sense, or even tautology.

From a learning and development perspective, the point of this tool is to understand better how learners think, behave and respond to different learning and development initiatives. This may be summarized in the following ways.

Linguistic intelligence is about being comfortable with words and language, as predominates in work roles that are about reading and writing, speaking and listening. Logical-mathematical intelligence is about using reasoning and deduction, and identifying patterns, as is common in science- and engineering-based roles, and involves extensive use of numbers. Musical intelligence is not just about responding to music, but about sound, tone and rhythm, and is about roles involving music and its broadest applications. Spatial intelligence is about heightened spatial and visual perception, as predominates in art and design, and anything involving the use of imagery. Bodily kinaesthetic intelligence is about physical coordination, including dexterity and agility, and predominates in active work roles involving touch, feel or physical movement. Interpersonal intelligence is about tuning into other people's feelings and is one of the two key things meant by emotional intelligence. Intrapersonal intelligence is the other aspect of emotional intelligence, focusing on self-awareness (see tool 13). Naturalist intelligence is about empathy with the natural environment. Existential or moral intelligence is about empathy with religious or ethical issues.

The practical application of all this is to consider these differing mindsets when identifying problems or challenges for learning and development, analysing needs and shaping solutions. Recognizing and responding to multiple intelligences are about playing to people's natural strengths, acknowledging and accepting different kinds of work behaviour that can contribute to goals and outcomes in different ways, working with different learning style preferences, and embracing and celebrating diversity.

FURTHER READING

Armstrong, T (2001) *7 Kinds of Smart: Identifying and developing your multiple intelligences*, Plume, New York
Gardner, H (1993) *Frames of Mind: The theory of multiple intelligences*, Basic Books, New York
Kagan, S and Kagan, M (2001) *Multiple Intelligences: The complete MI book*, Kagan Publishing, San Clemente, CA
http://www.howardgardner.com/
http://www.miinstitute.info/

Neuro-linguistic programming

20

X-REF TOOLS

11 Rose's learning styles

18 Emotional intelligence

19 Gardner's multiple intelligences

Neuro-linguistic programming, or NLP, was devised by Richard Bandler and John Grinder in 1975. It has little empirical evidence to substantiate its theory, and is thus still regarded with some scepticism in academic (psychological and linguistic) circles. However, it has had a significant impact on learning and development.

NLP is about influencing people: it is about understanding what motivates people and using that understanding to relate better to them, and to offer them services that better meet their needs. In the context of business, this fits with mainstream thinking about quality, customer care and accountability. In the context of learning and development, this is about focusing on learners' needs, interests and desires; it is a logical extension of learner-centred learning.

The core concept in NLP is modelling. The idea is to study what works well and model behaviour on that and, in interpersonal relationships, for the facilitator to model his or her behaviour on the learner's behaviour to the extent that it helps the facilitator gain the learner's trust and establish rapport.

There are four operational principles in NLP:

1 to focus on outcomes, and know what outcome to aim to achieve;

2 to have a clear understanding, or 'sensory acuity' in the NLP jargon, to recognize when one is moving towards or away from the outcome;

3 to have sufficient flexibility of behaviour to vary that behaviour until the outcome is achieved;

4 to recognize the time for action and to take it immediately.

On the face of it, this seems fairly prescriptive, but these are really just broad principles, to be varied in application, and NLP advocates offer substantial anecdotal evidence and case studies of their effectiveness in application. NLP has particular application to training, especially face-to-face training, interviewing, coaching and mentoring, and reviewing individuals' performance and development.

FURTHER READING

O'Connor, J and Seymour, J (2000) *Training with NLP (Neuro-Linguistic Programming): Skills for trainers*, managers and communicators, Thorsons, London

O'Connor, J and Seymour, J (2003) *Introducing NLP Neuro-Linguistic Programming*, Thorsons, London

Rajah, K and DeCoursey, A (2009) *Neuro Linguistic Programming: NLP for executive and professional development*, University of Greenwich, London

Ready, R and Burton, K (2010) *Neuro-Linguistic Programming for Dummies*, Wiley, Chichester

http://www.johngrinder.com/

http://www.nlpconference.co.uk/

http://www.richardbandler.com/

Knowledge management: distinguishing data, information and knowledge

---

21

X-REF TOOLS

37   The four phases of knowledge management
100   Evaluation: total value add

All organizations manage knowledge at some level, but it can be very difficult to distinguish potentially valuable information from worthless data, and it can pose a serious dilemma for an organization to decide what sort of knowledge is important and what isn't. Some organizations have resolved this dilemma by reference to a hierarchy of three, or sometimes four, levels:

1 *data*, which have little intrinsic value, but are easy to store;
2 *information*, which is data that have been interpreted, in order to measure their value or add some value;
3 *knowledge*, which is information that has been retained and developed by a person or people, who give it significant value and can turn it into an asset.

A possible fourth category is *wisdom*, arguably a higher form of knowledge, although here distinctions tend to become blurred.

Table 1.4 takes us through an example.

TABLE 1.4 Data, information and knowledge

Term	Definition	Illustrative example
Data	These are raw and unprocessed material that arrives from the external world. Feature little or no sorting, categorization or interpretation.	The receipt from a supermarket checkout, which transfers the prices of purchases into a simple table.
Information	Data that have been acted upon cognitively, codified, and transferred into a framework to be used for specific purposes.	If the supermarket has an automatic process of discounting, this can be shown at the bottom of the receipt as the total discount. This makes the data of some use to the customer.
Knowledge	The first point when a person or people have made a purposeful intervention in the process to give data or information a specific purpose or meaning.	The supermarket uses the information on the receipt to store purchasing histories for customers, develop lifestyle profiles, and predict future customer needs to help decide what products and promotions to offer.

Adapted from M Cope (1999) *Leading the Organisation to Learn*, FT Pitman, Harlow

The trouble with this classification is that it doesn't stand still. One person's data are another person's information. And even knowledge can deteriorate to data over time. As an example of the last circumstance, being able to predict the movement of a share price before it happens is very valuable knowledge, but knowing the price after it has moved is the crudest of data.

Another example could be that an employee's detailed understanding of a product or service, built up over many years of experience, may be reduced to a mark in a tick-box by somebody taking a survey of employees. It is knowledge to the specialist employee, but data to the surveyor.

What is important about this tool is that it may be used to identify the value of knowledge to the organization. Making a distinction between data, information and knowledge can help with this, but everyone should beware of a too rigid setting of boundaries. This tool can also inform our understanding of what may be learnt in an organization, can help with our analysis of organizational learning needs, and may contribute to our understanding of how value is added in the evaluation process.

FURTHER READING

Cope, M (1999) *Leading the Organisation to Learn*, FT Pitman, Harlow
Stewart, T (1997) *Intellectual Capital: The new wealth of organisations*, Nicholas Brealey, London

22

The five aspects of talent management

Talent management is a useful integrated model for viewing the continuous development of staff within an organization. The CIPD offers the following definitions: 'Talent consists of those individuals who can make a difference to organisational performance, either through their immediate contribution or in the longer term by demonstrating the highest levels of potential', and talent management is 'the systematic attraction, identification, development, engagement/retention and deployment of those individuals with high potential who are of particular value to an organisation' (from 'Talent management: design, implementation and evaluation', a CIPD member resource, July 2008).

The CIPD definition lists the five key aspects in an odd order, but they do overlap, and may be understood in the following terms:

- *Identifying* talent is about working out what sort of knowledge, skills, competences, attitudes and aptitudes an organization needs to achieve its goals now and in the future. It is also about working out where to find that talent, both in terms of where and how new employees may be recruited and in terms of how the organization may unearth the hidden talent within it.

- *Attracting* talent is not just about how recruitment is carried out, but about how the organization may be made a more attractive place to work. This includes the physical environment, the corporate culture, the way the organization is perceived both by employees and by the outside world, and the scope provided for people to learn, grow, find new challenges and develop their careers.

- *Deploying* talent is about working out how to make the most of people's talents, by setting them the right goals, placing them in the appropriate jobs, organizing them into appropriate work teams with an effective mix of people, and managing their performance to ensure that goals are achieved.

- *Developing* talent is about ensuring people have the opportunities to acquire the skills and expertise needed to fill current and future vacancies. Learning and development are concerned primarily with this aspect, but it is impossible to deal with it in isolation from the other four aspects. The catalogue of courses available in the training centre, the online learning environment, the learning resource centre, perhaps the corporate university, work-based learning initiatives, and coaching and mentoring schemes are all delivery mechanisms for developing talent.

- *Retaining* talent is about ensuring people continue to be engaged, challenged and stimulated in their work. It is about providing them with material rewards, resources to do their jobs, and personal support, and about ensuring that their career development needs are met. It is about ensuring that what is offered to them remains competitive with what they may be able to obtain elsewhere.

Talent management, in sum, is about implementing and integrating these five aspects as a coherent whole.

FURTHER READING

Berger, L and Berger, D (2003) *The Talent Management Handbook*, McGraw-Hill, New York

CIPD (2008) Talent management: design, implementation and evaluation, http://www.cipd.co.uk/subjects/recruitmen/general/_tlntmngttl. htm?IsSrchRes=1 (accessed November 2010 – full resource available to CIPD members only)

Davis, T (ed) (2007) *Talent Assessment: A new strategy for talent management*, Gower, Aldershot

Pellant, A and Thorne, K (2006) *The Essential Guide to Managing Talent: How top companies recruit, train and retain the best employees*, Kogan Page, London

http://www.talentmanagementreview.com

23   The talent web

X-REF TOOLS

22 The five aspects of talent management
24 The succession planning cycle
59 The seven pillars of a corporate university
82 Talent management and development: the GE nine box model

Talent management can sometimes seem a somewhat remote or theoretical process, but some key tools can bring it to life. One of these is a distinctive model devised by Andy Cross specifying the roles a manager needs to fulfil in order to be a talent manager. Cross calls his model the talent web.

The talent web describes five interrelated roles of:

- talent spotter;
- talent magnet;
- talent coach;
- talent blender; and
- talent conductor.

The first two of these roles – spotter and magnet – are about the first two aspects of a talent management strategy: identifying talent and attracting it. Managers responsible need to ask themselves what information, skills and resources they need in order to fulfil these roles.

The coach role is about the aspect of developing talent. There are many development options available to a manager, but the manager's role is about more than simply managing learning and development opportunities. It is about being a champion for talent management, and supporting others in encouraging learning and development. Talent managers need to ask themselves what they need to contribute to keep everyone on-strategy.

The role of talent blender is about the deployment aspect, and specifically about getting the right people to work together in the right way. It is about team building and fostering cooperation. Talent managers need to ask themselves what they can do to help put together and support effective teams.

The talent conductor works to ensure a flow of talented people, and this means building a profile of how everyone in the organization is performing and how that level of performance may be taken forward. This is about the management underpinning the talent management strategy. Talent managers need to ask themselves which people are performing well in their current roles and who can perform well in other roles in the future.

Figure 1.6 summarizes the roles of the talent manager in the talent web.

FIGURE 1.6   The talent web

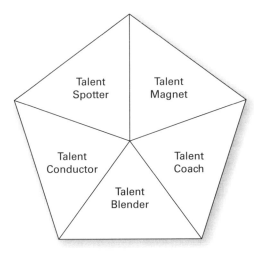

FURTHER READING

Cross, A (2007) *The Talent Management Pocketbook*, Management Pocketbooks, Alresford

24 The succession planning cycle

X-REF TOOLS

22 The five aspects of talent management

23 The talent web

54 How to mentor someone

One of the most significant aspects of talent management, as identified in tool 22, is succession planning. This is the means whereby employees are groomed to move into the roles their organization will need them to fill at some point in the near future. Succession planning may be viewed as a cycle, comprising a sequence of four phases: clarify the development needs, or the roles to fill; identify the possible successors to those roles; develop and prepare those successors; promote and compensate them. This is shown in Figure 1.7.

In its crudest form, succession planning may be applied to a hierarchy in which promising subordinates are supported and prepared to step up into the next most senior role when their time comes. Succession planning is often associated with the identification and development of top performers, people with high potential, mentoring and shadowing schemes, and fast-track routes to senior positions.

However, it is a limiting mindset to assume that people simply want to be promoted to the highest level they can attain in their organization. In many of today's flatter organizational structures, such continued vertical progression is not even possible. Increasingly, people are looking for different kinds of challenges, recognition, rewards and fulfilment in their work. The consequence of this is that effective talent management is about finding out what people want and what motivates them, and mapping that to the needs of the organization, both now and in the future. The cycle accommodates this broader perspective, and may be applied as a tool to help the broader process.

FIGURE 1.7 The succession planning cycle

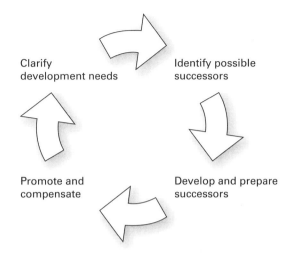

Clarify
development needs

Identify possible
successors

Promote and
compensate

Develop and prepare
successors

FURTHER READING

Cannon, J and McGee, R (2007) *Talent Management and Succession Planning*, CIPD Toolkit, CIPD, London

Rothwell, W (2010) *Effective Succession Planning: Ensuring leadership continuity and building talent from within*, Amacom, New York

Sims, D and Gay, M (2007) *Building Tomorrow's Talent: A practitioner's guide to talent management and succession planning*, AuthorHouse, Bloomington, IN

25 Devising and using standards of competence

X-REF TOOLS

71 Assessing and recording competence

84 Applying quality management tools to learning

The time-honoured method of learning how to accomplish a task is to break it down into small steps, or stages, and master each of them in turn. Similarly, learning and development professionals have always sought to break down the components of a job or task in order to prepare training plans. For many years, a training officer's staple was skills analysis and job analysis; the former broke a job or task down into the skills that had to be learnt to accomplish it, while the latter broke the job down into its component functions, for the same purpose.

In the 1980s, these analyses began to be superseded by considerations of competence or competency. (The two terms are essentially synonymous, though pedantic attempts have been made to distinguish them.) The roots of this go back much further, but it was after Richard Boyatzis popularized the concept in 1982 that it became much more commonplace. In the UK, it was the Manpower Services Commission, a government body, that in 1986 defined occupational competence as 'the ability to perform activities in the jobs within an occupation, to the standards expected in employment', and this definition became the basis of the UK National Occupational Standards movement, and was adopted by Investors in People in 1991.

Essentially competence is the application of the necessary knowledge, skills and attitudes to fulfil a job function. More precisely, this is functional competence, which specifies functions, or outcomes, as its units of competence, as distinct from behavioural competence, which specifies processes, or behavioural skills, as its units of competence. Functional competence traces its origins back to job analysis; behavioural competence traces its origins back to skills analysis. Both have their uses but, in the UK at least, functional competence has prevailed, because of its outcome focus and its capacity to shape job standards and National Occupational Standards.

Controversy continues over the contrasting of an absolute sense of competence with its opposite, incompetence, and some argue that competence should be seen as a continuum, along which learners may move, acquiring incremental degrees of competence. Others dispute the limitations of competence, arguing that setting minimum standards limits performance potential, and calling for a sort of 'competence-plus', or excellence, as a more worthwhile and stretching goal. Further confusion arises over the use of the term 'core competence' by Gary Hamel and C K Prahalad, articulated in their 1994 book *Competing for the Future*; their concept of organizational core competence as the lever of competitive advantage is quite different from the model of individual competence we are concerned with here.

Most common occupations in the UK, from accounting to zoology, are now defined by a set of National Occupational Standards, and these in turn form the basis of not just job design, but teaching and training programmes to meet job needs, and qualification outcomes, notably the National Vocational Qualifications, or NVQs (in Scotland, SVQs). These latter uses are the main area of interest for learning and development professionals.

National Occupational Standards are broken down into standards, or units of competence, which are then subdivided into elements of competence. These units and elements are measured by performance criteria, which specify how the learner's competence may be measured in some detail, defining the range and scope of activities that may demonstrate the criteria, and specifying the acceptable evidence requirements.

However, no matter how thorough this process, there remain many occupations outside the scope of National Occupational Standards, and some where a manager may prefer to develop a variant, or completely different version, to suit local or organization-specific needs. Such local action remains valid, as long as it follows the same disciplined approach used by the National Occupational Standards.

FURTHER READING

Barbazette, J (2005) *The Trainer's Journey to Competence: Tools, assessments, and models*, Jossey-Bass, San Francisco

Boyatzis, R (1982) *The Competent Manager: Model for effective performance*, Wiley, New York

Eraut, M (1994) *Developing Professional Knowledge and Competence*, Routledge, London

Hamel, G and Prahalad, CK (1994) *Competing for the Future*, Harvard Business School Press, US

Winterton, J and Winterton, R (1999) *Developing Managerial Competence*, Routledge, London

http://www.investorsinpeople.co.uk

http://www.ukstandards.org.uk

26 Board-level development: a needs audit

X-REF TOOLS

   4   Identifying organizational learning needs: a step-by-step approach
  24   The succession planning cycle

Nearly all of the tools in this book could, in theory at least, be applied to almost any organization in any work setting; there are a couple of exceptions and this is one, included because it is such a significant exception. This tool is of value only to organizations that have a board of directors or equivalent, although others may find some application for it. The tool is basically a classification of questions to ask when auditing the learning and development needs of members of a board of directors or equivalent senior team.

The questions fall into four categories:

1 understanding the organization;

2 the board's working practices;

3 directors' behaviours;

4 responsiveness to stakeholders.

This model offers 20 questions, a set of five for each category, but more may be added or some of these excluded; this is not a comprehensive taxonomy of questions, merely a representative selection of what may be useful:

Understanding the organization:

1 Have board members undertaken induction and further formal learning and development on how the business operates?

2 Do board members share a common understanding of the organization that is accurate and up to date?

3 Do board members have a shared understanding of their main responsibilities and of how success will be measured?

4 Does the board conduct a thoroughgoing review of business performance?

5 Does the board receive regular feedback on the implementation of important decisions?

The board's working practices:

6 Are there processes in place to enable board members to participate in strategy formulation?

7 Do board members monitor the implementation of strategy?

8 Do board members have a consistent process for considering business proposals?

9 Do board members review financial reports in accordance with their fiduciary responsibilities?

10 Are mechanisms in place enabling board members to benchmark their performance against board members in other organizations?

Directors' behaviours:

11 Do board members play an active part in board proceedings, and account for their actions and those of the staff who report to them?

12 Is there a balance of contribution between the executive and non-executive directors?

13 Do board members work together as a team?

14 Does each board member have a personal development plan?

15 Do board members exchange feedback on their respective performances?

Responsiveness to stakeholders:

16 Are all board members exposed to a range of views from shareholders, employees and other stakeholders in the business?

17 Does the board take into account public opinion and the organization's reputation?

18 Do board members report regularly on their work to various communities of stakeholders?

19 Do stakeholders feel the board is representing their interests satisfactorily?

20 Do board members have working relationships with the external auditors?

Finally, the process here, which is derived from the guidelines of the Audit Commission, may be applied to other work teams, departments, divisions or layers of management within an organization. With a few changes to the structure and/or the range of questions, the tool may be adapted to a number of related purposes.

FURTHER READING

Bain, N (2007) *The Effective Director: Building individual and board success*, Kogan Page, London

Institute of Directors (2002) *Standards for the Board: Improving the effectiveness of your board (Good practice for directors)*, Kogan Page, London

Learning methods and styles grid

X-REF TOOLS

10 Honey and Mumford's learning styles

49 Reference list of learning and development methods

Table 1.5 charts how well various learning methods fit with different learning styles. The four styles considered are those identified by Honey and Mumford, after Kolb.

TABLE 1.5 Learning methods and styles grid

	Activist	Reflector	Theorist	Pragmatist
Didactic coursework	x	~	~	~
Participative coursework	⌐	~	~	~
Attending conferences	x	⌐	⌐	
Attending exhibitions	~	~		⌐
Playing games	⌐			
Watching videos	x	⌐	⌐	
Psychometrics	x	⌐	⌐	~
Outdoor development	⌐			~

TABLE 1.5 *Continued*

	Activist	Reflector	Theorist	Pragmatist
Open/distance learning	]	]	]	]
e-learning	]	]	]	]
Resource-based learning		]	]	
Assessment techniques	~	]		]
Development centres	]	]	]	]
'Sitting-by-Nellie'	]	~	x	~
On-the-job instruction	]			~
Secondment	]	~	~	~
Coaching/mentoring		]	]	~
Action learning	]		x	]
Work-based learning	~	~	]	~
Performance review		]	~	]
Learning records		]		
Discovery learning	]			]

Key:
] indicates a good fit
x indicates a poor fit
~ indicates a possible good fit
no mark indicates neutrality

Activists tend to prefer participative coursework, games, outdoor development, activity-based flexible learning, practical exercises in development
centres, on-the-job activities like 'sitting-by-Nellie', instruction/demonstra-
tion (with practice) and discovery learning, secondments, team building and
action learning.

Reflectors tend to prefer attending conferences, watching videos, using
psychometric instruments, studying the content of open/distance learning
and e-learning programmes, resource-based learning, formal assessments

(including those that take place in development centres), coaching, performance and development reviews, and the use of learning records.

Theorists tend to prefer lectures, conferences, videos, psychometric instruments, the content of open/distance learning and e-learning programmes, resource-based learning, the broader, conceptual aspects of development centres and work-based projects, and coaching, at least at a theoretical level.

Pragmatists tend to prefer exhibitions, activities offered in distance learning and e-learning programmes (that can be tested at the workplace), some assessments and related aspects of development centres, team building, action learning, performance and development reviews and discovery learning.

FURTHER READING

Honey, P and Mumford, A (1982) *Manual of Learning Styles*, Peter Honey
    Publications, Maidenhead
Kolb, D A (1983) *Experiential Learning: Experience as the source of
    learning and development*, FT Prentice Hall, Harlow

28 Learning methods choice matrix

X-REF TOOLS

27 Learning methods and styles grid

33 Using different approaches to learning and development

49 Reference list of learning and development methods

There are several criteria to be considered when choosing an appropriate learning method. Tool 27 mapped each of the main learning methods against individual learner style preferences, but there are other equally important criteria.

Some methods for learning and development may be better suited to individual learning, while some may be better suited to group work, and some work for both. Some learning methods may be utilized on the job, while some are for an off-the-job setting.

Bringing together these two dimensions, we can construct a two-by-two matrix, plotting individual or group work methods against on- or off-the-job methods. This can help simplify the choice to be made. See Figure 1.8.

It is perhaps striking that there are relatively few methods available for groups to learn on the job, but the work itself is arguably the means whereby groups of employees learn together to be better at what they do, or perhaps it points to the need for more attention to this area. In any case, this matrix is only a guide. It cannot make the decision for the manager responsible; it is just a tool to clarify some of the issues, hopefully a useful tool.

FIGURE 1.8 Learning methods choice matrix

	Group-work	Individual
Off-the-job	Courses Games Videos Outdoor development Open, flexible and distance learning e-learning Development centres	Games Videos Psychometrics Open, flexible and distance learning e-learning Resource-based learning Assessment techniques
On-the-job	Team development Action learning Work-based projects Learning records Discovery learning	'Sitting-by-Nellie' Instruction Guided practice Secondment Coaching & mentoring Work-based projects Personal development plans

FURTHER READING

Grubb, W N (1996) *Learning to Work: The case for reintegrating job training and education*, Russell Sage Foundation, New York

PART TWO
Planning learning

This part of the book considers a range of 21 tools that contribute to planning learning.

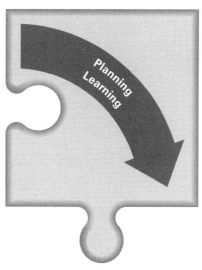

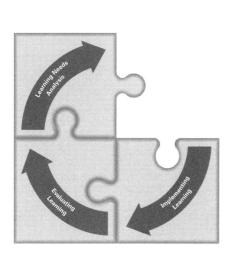

The six essential elements of a learning strategy

29

X-REF TOOLS

4 Identifying organizational learning needs:
a step-by-step approach

49 Reference list of learning and development methods

59 The seven pillars of a corporate university

89 Evaluation: how to recognize and when to use the main methods

A learning strategy is a compass guiding the pursuit of learning and development activities within an organization; it is a means of ensuring that they pursue a predetermined course to meet organizational objectives, in keeping with organizational values. Such a strategy is an invaluable tool for learning and development professionals to ensure their efforts are well aimed, meaningful and consistent. The six essential elements of a learning strategy are as follows:

1 *Scope.* The strategy should clarify what it covers (and perhaps what it doesn't cover), what it understands by learning in the organization's context, and how the learning strategy aligns with HR strategy, overall business strategy and all other strategies within the organization. It should provide shared understanding.

2 *Aims and objectives.* The strategy should include a clear statement of aims and objectives, recognizably linked to more general aims and objectives for the organization. This may or may not be expressed in an explicit mission statement, but regardless should reflect the corporate values and culture and should be written in the corporate style and language. It should provide a shared vision.

3 *Planning framework.* The strategy document needs to provide a framework for action plans, project work, quality management and

other initiatives – it needs to provide practical guidance to everyone involved in learning and development. It should provide a shared way of working.

4 *Resources and partners.* The strategy needs to consider the resourcing of learning and development, and the partners involved in this. These will include: all learners and their managers; senior management, who will wish to influence learning; tangential functions such as IT or knowledge management; potentially interested parties from the wider community, such as shareholders, customers, families of employees, and others; and last, but by no means least, external suppliers. It should clarify who and what is involved.

5 *Methods and approaches.* The strategy needs to set out the ways in which learning and development will be delivered in the organization, such as classroom delivery, work-based learning, e-learning, coaching and other methods. This need not be a limiting list, but should give a sense of how learning works in the organization. It should provide a common approach.

6 *Evaluation.* Lastly, the strategy needs to spell out how it will prove the worth of learning and development to the organization. It should specify the preferred approach to the evaluation of learning and development and how this will affect participants in the process. It should show how results will be measured.

FURTHER READING

Cartwright, R (2003) *Developing and Implementing a Training and Development Strategy*, Capstone, Oxford

Mayo, A (2004) *Creating a Learning and Development Strategy: The HR business partner's guide to developing people*, CIPD, London

Morrison, D (2005) *E-Learning Strategies*, Wiley, Chichester

Using the learning and development cycle to plan learning interventions

X-REF TOOLS

3 L&DNA grids
4 Identifying organizational learning needs: a step-by-step approach
5 Performance analysis quadrant

The learning and development cycle's four phases, described in more detail in tool 1, are usually represented in a circular, or cyclical, diagram: identifying and analysing learning needs; planning and preparation of the learning; delivery of the learning; and assessment, evaluation and review of the learning. The same four phases may be used as a planning cycle, to plan learning interventions:

- *Phase one: identifying and analysing learning needs.* This may include collation and study of information from individual performance reviews, employee surveys, managers' reports, suggestion schemes, business reviews, customer feedback and other sources, including not least the outcomes of phase four (below) for previous implementations. The analysis should seek to identify common issues, patterns, trends, and issues of major urgency or importance. Only by initially completing this phase can an organization hope to address the other phases in a meaningful way.

- *Phase two: planning and preparation of the learning.* This may include selecting the people who will undertake the learning, selecting the resources to use, selecting any service suppliers, determining a timescale, perhaps producing a project plan in the organization's preferred format (eg a flow chart) or using the organization's preferred project management software, designing the learning, and completing all the final preparations such as issuing joining instructions. All of this is an essential precondition for phase three.

- *Phase three: delivery of the learning.* This phase should hopefully be self-explanatory – actually running the learning intervention. This should include the support arrangements (facilitators, mentors, the role of line managers, peer support from other learners, etc) and a feedback loop to check that pre-designed learning components, such as pre-course work, are actually delivering what they are supposed to do. This leads into phase four.

- *Phase four: assessment, evaluation and review of the learning.* The learning needs to be assessed in terms of learners' feelings or reactions to it. How learners perform against the learning objectives needs to be measured; how the learning performs against the objectives the organization sets for it should also be measured, and this may be planned both in respect of learners' subsequent behaviour at work and in respect of wider organizational benefits.

This four-phase approach may be applied to anything from courses to work-based learning, and from coaching to e-learning; the principles are applicable to any kind of learning intervention.

FURTHER READING

Rae, L (1997) *Planning and Designing Training Programmes*, Gower, Aldershot

A step-by-step guide to planning a learning event

X-REF TOOLS

There are eight steps to follow when planning a learning event – a course or any other face-to-face learning intervention – to improve the prospects of the event being successful.

The first step is to consider the learners. Clarify who they are and how many there are. Confirm their learning needs. Check whether any of them have any additional, personal needs. Try to establish what their learning style preferences are, and how they have responded to previous learning events.

The second step is to consider the aim or purpose of the event, and focus in on the learner objectives. Set them or, if they have already been set, review them. Consider how they may best be met.

The third step is the choice of learning event itself. Choose an appropriate approach and method, such as a coaching session or a classroom-based course. Consider the best way for it to be delivered.

The fourth step is about timing. Consider how much time learners may have available and how long they will need to spend to complete the learning. Construct a timetable.

The fifth step is to carry out briefings. Decide who needs to be involved to facilitate the learning, such as a trainer or coach, and how many of these facilitators will be needed. Consider who else needs to be kept informed, such as line managers. Then make sure everybody is fully briefed.

The sixth step is preparation. Make sure all of the practical preparations for the event are made, such as the booking of premises and provision of facilities, equipment and materials. Tool 61 provides a detailed checklist for a course.

The seventh step is monitoring. Review everything that is happening, before, during and after the event, and have contingency plans in place for anything that may be anticipated to go wrong.

The eighth and final (but not necessarily the last) step is evaluation. This is really one of the first things to consider, and is certainly part of the advance planning. Determine in advance how the success of the learning event is to be measured, and ensure measures are taken at appropriate times in the process. Maintain records to inform future learning event planning.

FURTHER READING

Dearling, A (2003) *Organising Successful Learning Events: A guide to planning and running conferences, seminars and workshops for anyone involved in facilitating training in the people services*, Russell House Publishing, Lyme Regis

http://www.rnao.org/Storage/12/661_BPG_educators_resource_chapter_3.pdf (accessed December 2010)

Personal development planning

X-REF TOOLS

22 The five aspects of talent management
71 Assessing and recording competence
72 Learning logs and contracts

Personal development plans are tools for creating and pursuing learning and progression routes based on self-awareness, reflection, goal setting and planning for personal and career development. Their use is not limited to business organizations, but it is here that they find a role for aligning individuals' development planning with the needs of their organizations.

Personal development planning is often conducted within the context of periodic performance and development reviews, but may also be a stand-alone activity.

The principle is simple. The learner identifies exactly what he or she wants to attain, then specifies this in the form of personal development goals, defines the activities that will lead to these goals being met, and allocates appropriate time, resources and support. The format may vary, but the principle remains the same: the learner sets targets and the means to accomplish them.

Organizations harness this by sharing a common format among all employees, and coordinating this activity by establishing a cycle for individuals to complete their personal development plans around the same time. These personal development plans may then be aggregated to create organizational learning plans, to identify common themes to be addressed by training activities, and to find cost-effective solutions to the more individualized needs.

A key issue in getting started with a personal development plan is to have a structure for identifying the development needs. A map of the organization's needs for the roles it has created could address this. A common approach is to devise a suite of competences for the organization; in the UK, a set of National Occupational Standards can provide this. Using either of these starting points, the learner takes each section or area of competence that may be relevant to him or her and builds the plan from there.

In the absence of an organizational structure, individuals could use SWOT analysis, or a similar simple tool, to identify their strengths and weaknesses.

The plan could go on to identify inputs required, sources of support, timescales to tackle the development needs, resources, contacts, budgets, or anything else that may be necessary to pursue a course of development within the organization. Personal development planning may thus be as simple or as complex as an organization wishes it to be.

FURTHER READING

Cottrell, S (2003) *Skills for Success: The personal development planning handbook*, Palgrave Macmillan, Houndmills

Mumford, A (2001) *How to Produce Personal Development Plans*, Peter Honey Publications, Maidenhead

Murdock, A and Scutt, C (2002) *Personal Effectiveness*, Butterworth-Heinemann, Oxford

Sangster, C (2000) *Planning and Organising Personal and Professional Development*, Gower, Aldershot

http://www.businesslink.gov.uk/bdotg/action/pdp

Using different approaches to learning and development

33

There are many different ways of thinking about learning, and countless different methods or techniques for applying that thinking. Yet there are just a small number of approaches to learning. An approach may be defined as the way the learning is tackled, from a delivery perspective. Within many organizations there is a strong preference for one particular approach; for example, some organizations have a marked preference for learning on the job, while others place great stock in sending employees to attend courses, and companies based on digital technologies often prefer to use e-learning. Another way of viewing learning approaches is as clusters, or sets, of learning methods or techniques.

The six main approaches are as follows:

1 *On-the-job learning* is the generic term for the range of methods deployed to help learners learn in situ, in the work situation, while they are actually doing the job. This approach has the advantage that

there is no need for learning transfer to the real work situation, as that is where the learning has actually been undertaken.

2 *Coursework* describes the range of learning methods deployed in the classroom, and in the context of learning for work includes workshops, tutorial groups, seminars, lectures and all expressions of learning in a group situation, off the job.

3 *e-learning* is the collective term for all of the ways of supporting learning that draw upon digital technology. See tool 39 for more information.

4 *Resource-based learning* embraces all forms of learning using materials, publications and other resources, such as specialist training equipment and simulators.

5 *Coaching, mentoring and other learning alliances* (counselling, guardianship, etc) are a range of methods that make up this approach, and are usually intensive one-to-one means of support.

6 *Innovative approaches* to learning are those that are new and innovative to the learner, and seek to capitalize on this advantage. Of course, what is new and innovative to some may be old hat to others. The idea of the innovative approach is to capture the imagination, engage the learners with something that excites them, and build the learning from there. This will only work if the approach is truly innovative.

All of the learning methods in the reference list in tool 49 may be classified under one of these approaches.

FURTHER READING

There is a dearth of literature on this subject. Most searches lead to texts on ways of learning, and approaches taken by learners. An interesting discussion of the background is F Newman and L Holzman (1997) *The End of Knowing: A new developmental way of learning*, Routledge, London

Criteria for choosing a learning approach

34

X-REF TOOL

33 Using different approaches to learning and development

When choosing a learning approach, there are five criteria to measure each possible approach against, as shown in Figure 2.1, and these should be considered in the order below:

1 *Learning needs*. The first, inescapable criterion is to identify the learning needs. It may be possible for these to be addressed by any learning approach, but it may be that one in particular, or a small selection, is strongly suggested by the needs. There may be ways in which the learning lends itself to a particular approach. It is likely that most learning needs can be addressed by a variety of approaches, but some may require a special approach and, if so, the rest of these five criteria can be ignored, as the issue of meeting learning needs should have primacy. This is about the purpose of the learning, and about maintaining a learner-centred perspective.

2 *Learner style preferences*. If it is known, then account needs to be taken of how the learners like to learn; and, if it's not known, some effort should be expended on finding out. It may be possible for the learning solution to take account of these preferences. Bear in mind that different learning approaches can appeal in different ways to different learning style preferences. The more the learners enjoy and are engaged in the learning, the more likely the learning will be successful. This continues the learner-centred perspective.

3 *Cost*. By the time the third criterion is considered, there is probably already a shortlist of possible approaches. These may be reduced by comparing their costs. Estimates should be sufficient to determine which approach should be least costly; linking with criterion 5

(below) should help to determine which approach would be most cost-effective.

4 *Time*. There may be some time pressure on implementing the learning: it may be urgent. A further consideration is how long roll-out of learning will take using different approaches.

5 *Adding value*. The fifth criterion is to consider how the learning is going to be evaluated. How will its impact be measured? This will probably influence the learning approach.

FIGURE 2.1 Criteria for choosing a learning approach

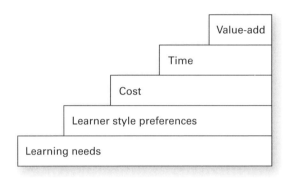

Once all five criteria have been considered, it is likely just one possible learning approach will be left. If there is still a choice, then a decision may be made by whatever other criteria may be relevant, or the choice may be offered to someone else, perhaps a senior manager or sponsor – or perhaps the learners themselves could have the opportunity to choose.

FURTHER READING

Reeve, F, Cartwright, M and Edwards, R (eds) (2001) *Supporting Lifelong Learning*, vol 2: *Organising Learning*, Routledge, London

Sloman, M (2007) *The Changing World of the Trainer: Emerging good practice*, Butterworth-Heinemann, Oxford

A checklist for procuring learning services

35

X-REF TOOLS

36 Outsourcing versus insourcing

44 Checklist – 10 things to look out for when dealing with e-learning vendors

45 What to look for in a learning and development consultant

88 How to get value from learning consultants

Procuring learning services from outside the organization is fraught with difficulties and dangers. The following is a checklist of 10 factors to consider when engaging in procurement:

1 Is the service really needed? This may seem self-evident, but the whole issue needs to be thought out in advance, to avoid wasting everyone's time in embarking on a process that may have to be aborted when it comes to light that the service is not actually needed after all.

2 If the need is established, does the service have to be procured externally, or does the organization have the resources to provide the service in-house? External procurement can be expensive and time-consuming, and should be initiated only once other avenues have been explored.

3 Once committed to external procurement, who are the potential vendors, and what sources of information can point to likely vendors? If the supply side of the market is unknown, this can be an invaluable phase, during which informal discussions may be held with potential vendors, to help clarify what sort of businesses they are and what sort of services they provide.

4 What is the overall procurement process, and who is responsible for it? This is essentially a project, and should be managed as such, with a dedicated project manager and a project plan to deliver the desired outcome – successful procurement of the service.

5 How should the opportunity be advertised? What are the best channels and media for reaching vendors? And what points should be highlighted in the advertising?

6 What specification should be provided to prospective suppliers? The details are important in helping vendors decide whether or not to bid for the work and in narrowing the field to specialists with the expertise and resources to meet the procurement specification.

7 How will the shortlisting be conducted, and what criteria will be used? This should be determined before any bids are considered, to ensure objectivity; otherwise there is a danger that the process is used simply to justify a decision that has already been made, perhaps instinctively but without due consideration of all the facts.

8 How will the selection decision be made, and how will it be communicated to both the successful bidder and the unsuccessful bidders?

9 Is there a contract in place to offer to the successful vendor? This should be sorted out in advance.

10 What happens next? Is a plan in place to move seamlessly from the vendor selection to contracting to service delivery?

Procurement is a specialized process, and the larger the scale of the procurement, or the bigger the investment, the more likely it is that specialist input will be required. If the organization has a procurement or purchasing function, this is a job for them, in conjunction with whoever wants to procure the learning service(s). If not, then hopefully this checklist can provide a guide for a non-specialist to conduct small-scale procurement.

FURTHER READING

van Adelsberg, D and Trolley, E (1999) *Running Training like a Business: Delivering unmistakable value*, Berrett-Koehler, San Francisco

Outsourcing versus insourcing

X-REF TOOLS

This tool addresses the common dilemma about whether to meet learning needs from internal resources or to draw upon the resources of an external provider. The latter option has for some time been described as 'outsourcing'; more recently, the alternative has been called 'insourcing'. Some, like Walton (1999), describe the options as a continuum, with outsourcing at one end, insourcing at the other, but intermediate options offering a blend of the two. Walton uses the terms 'out-tasking' and 'intasking', and defines his full suite of four terms dynamically, with reference to what has changed (eg services previously provided by external providers being brought in-house).

There is a much wider debate about this subject (see 'Further reading' below), but for this tool, in the context of learning and development, we are concerned simply with the decision about whether to go in-house or out of house.

None of the many attempts to establish a theoretical framework for this decision is definitive. Some stress the distinction between the core and peripheral activities of an organization, suggesting the latter may more readily be outsourced, but not the former. Core activities could include coordinating learning needs analyses and personal development plans for the organization; peripheral activities could include provision of training in generic skills such as using standard IT applications. Others cite Michael Porter's value chain analysis, in distinguishing primary and support activities: again, the suggestion is that support activities may more readily be outsourced than primary activities, although in our context all learning and development could be seen as support activities, and so this distinction is not particularly helpful.

A simple rule of thumb is to compare the relative costs of internal and external provision, but better is to compare cost-effectiveness, or better still the total value added.

The matrix in Figure 2.2 summarizes the relative advantages and disadvantages of each approach.

FIGURE 2.2   Outsourcing/insourcing matrix

	Outsourcing	**Insourcing**
Advantages	• Access to greater specialist expertise • Converts fixed costs to variable costs • Conserves in-house resources • More flexible	• Maximizes use of existing resources • Enables organisation to concentrate on core expertise • Greater control over activities • Easier to manage
Disadvantages	• Lack of in-house resources • Lack of in-house expertise • Potential for over-reliance on a supplier • Less influence over supplier service levels	• Constrains existing resources • Keeps costs as fixed overheads • Misses out on expertise outside the organization • Less flexible

Of course, outsourcing and insourcing are not necessarily opposites, nor mutually exclusive. The middle ground lies in collaboration, such as when external consultants work alongside the organization's learning and development staff. This approach can succeed in instances where the advantages in the upper half of Figure 2.2 outweigh the disadvantages in the lower half.

FURTHER READING

Corbett, M (2010) *The Outsourcing Revolution: Why it makes sense and how to do it right*, Kaplan, Chicago

Silverstein, D, DeCarlo, N and Slocum, M (2007) *Insourcing Innovation: How to achieve competitive excellence using TRIZ*, Auerbach Publications, Boca Raton, FL

Walton, J (1999) *Outsourcing: what stays in and what goes out*, Ch 11 in *Strategic Human Resource Development*, FT Prentice Hall, Harlow

http://hr.toolbox.com/wiki/index.php/Learning_and_development_outsourcing (accessed December 2010)

37 The four phases of knowledge management

X-REF TOOLS

15 How to develop a learning organization

21 Knowledge management: distinguishing data, information and knowledge

100 Evaluation: total value add

Knowledge management is a broad theoretical concept that may be converted into a practical tool for learning and development professionals; it is about making the most of the talents of employees by getting their know-how to work for the organization, turning individual capabilities into collective assets.

If we are to manage knowledge successfully, we need to consider four distinct but complementary phases:

1 creating knowledge;
2 accumulating knowledge;
3 storing and retrieving knowledge;
4 applying knowledge.

Closer study of these four phases, and recognition of their distinction, can help shape learning and development solutions that better meet needs and have a more lasting legacy:

- *Creating knowledge.* People are constantly creating knowledge: the challenge for the organization that employs them is to harness it. There are broadly two sorts of things organizations can do to achieve this: one is to encourage individuals to undertake research, original work and self-development, and to collaborate with others in these activities; and the other is to put in place an organizational structure that encourages knowledge creation – a learning organization.

- *Accumulating knowledge.* This phase is about gathering together all the knowledge that people have and that the organization has gathered over time. One of the fundamental assumptions of knowledge management is that many organizations don't do this, or do it poorly, and thus are not benefiting enough from the knowledge they have already generated. Software systems can help with this.

- *Storing and retrieving knowledge.* This phase goes hand in hand with accumulating knowledge. It's about retaining and manipulating the organization's knowledge and, again, can be facilitated by software systems. Accumulating, sorting and retrieving knowledge have had a lot of attention, especially from technologists offering solutions, but this can often be like hyperlinked, hypersonic librarianship. More of learning and development's focus should be on the phases of creating and applying knowledge.

- *Applying knowledge.* In order to derive the maximum benefit from any learning activity – or, to put it another way, any knowledge-creating activity – it is essential to have a plan in place to apply the new knowledge. This is where we realize the value from learning and knowledge – in product innovation, in organizational effectiveness and in customer service. Knowledge application is the natural corollary of knowledge creation.

FURTHER READING

Fee, K (2000) Creating value from knowledge, *Management Scotland,* May, http://www.learnforever.co.uk/articles/Creating_Value_from_ Knowledge.pdf

38 The three component parts of e-learning

X-REF TOOLS

2 Understanding learning, development, education and training

39 The five models of e-learning

E-learning, in all its forms, including all applications of digital technology to learning, and including combinations of digital and non-digital forms (sometimes described as blended learning), may be better understood by breaking it down into its three component parts:

- enabling technology;
- learning content; and
- learning design.

This is illustrated by Figure 2.3.

People tend to focus on the first, the technology, because for many this is the relatively new and unfamiliar component, but the other two are at least as important. Software vendors tend to place great emphasis on the first, because that is what they contribute and where they make their money, but that doesn't mean learning and development professionals ought to do the same.

Getting the content right is, of course, very important in any learning intervention, e-learning included. But this can lead people to overemphasize it, as encapsulated in the often-heard phrase 'Content is king'. It's not.

Technologists often underestimate what's involved in the process of learning, seeing it as little more than manipulation of content. And sometimes vendors emphasize the primacy of content to flatter the buyer or to protect

FIGURE 2.3   The three component parts of e-learning

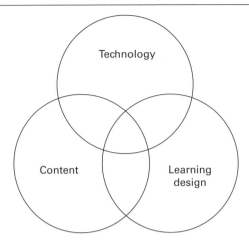

their technology. Their concept of learning is as a process for transferring knowledge from A to B, like the traditional, simple, sender–receiver model for communication. This is a good formula for providing information online, but there's a lot more to learning than just providing information.

The 'lot more' is the third component, learning design, sometimes also referred to as pedagogy. Effective learning design is about applying thinking about how people learn, and how best to manage the learning process to achieve improved performance at work. For learning and development professionals, arguably, the design component is the most important of the three.

E-learning can sometimes seem a bit mysterious, especially to those un-familiar with digital technology and its accompanying jargon. This simple tool can greatly aid the process of demystification.

FURTHER READING

Fee, K (2009) *Delivering E-Learning*, Kogan Page, London
Morrison, D (2005) *E-Learning Strategies*, Wiley, Chichester
Sloman, M (2002) *The E-Learning Revolution*, CIPD, London
http://www.brandon-hall.com
http://www.masieweb.com

39 The five models of e-learning

X-REF TOOLS

33 Using different approaches to learning and development

38 The three component parts of e-learning

41 The route map model for e-learning design

77 Blended learning models

78 Social networking and collaborative tools

E-learning may be defined as an approach to learning and development: a collection of tools and techniques utilizing digital technologies, which enable, distribute and enhance learning. But within this definition there are many learning methods we can include under the broad sweep of e-learning, such as undertaking online courses, practising simulations, reading and viewing online learning resources, taking part in online discussion forums, etc.

To make sense of the array of e-learning methods, we need to recognize that there are a number of different models, all of which have their uses. There are five identified so far, shown in Table 2.1, but there may be more that could come to light with the development of new technologies or new working practices.

Model 1, online courses, is what most people think of when they consider e-learning, and is probably the most common model. When it is combined with offline activities, it becomes model 2, which is sometimes called blended learning (although blending is really what learners do themselves, in all models – a better term for this would be 'blended training').

Model 3 is useful for continuous professional development (CPD) schemes and for informal and non-formal learning, and provides a looser framework that may be attractive to more experienced learners.

TABLE 2.1 The five models of e-learning

Model 1	Online courses	Purely online courses, which provide learning solely via the internet.
Model 2	Integrated online and offline learning, or 'blended learning'	Learning programmes that integrate online learning with complementary offline activities.
Model 3	Self-managed e-learning	The provision of online learning resources for self-managed learning.
Model 4	Live e-learning	Synchronous online learning events, involving learners in multiple locations.
Model 5	Electronic performance support (EPS)	Work-based online learning to support specific tasks, systems or operational procedures.

Model 4 has evolved from videoconferencing and 'webinars' (online seminars) and allows simultaneous learning events to take place across different locations.

Model 5 has evolved from the application of digital technologies to performance support systems. It typically involves support systems, rather like instruction manuals, based on desktop computers or on handheld devices.

All of these models could be delivered via any kind of computer interface, including handhelds. Thus what some call 'mobile learning' is not another model, but a delivery mechanism for any of the existing five.

One of the benefits of recognizing these models is that it allows the manager to consider different ways of supporting learners to match different situations and needs. Another benefit is that it helps better explain the use of digital technology for learning, and avoids misunderstandings about what e-learning allegedly can or can't do.

Some of these models can be very expensive to implement, but there are usually budget versions available, especially with the growth of free and open source software. The real costs are likely to lie in familiarizing learners, and those who support them, with the models, and how they work, rather than just in acquiring and installing the technology.

FURTHER READING

Fee, K (2009) *Delivering E-Learning*, Kogan Page, London
Morrison, D, *E-Learning Strategies*, Wiley, Chichester
Rossett, A (ed) (2002) *The ASTD E-Learning Handbook: Best practices, strategies and case studies for an emerging field*, McGraw-Hill, New York
Sloman, M (2003) *Training in the Age of the Learner*, CIPD, London

Learning design: the five dimensions

X-REF TOOLS

2 Understanding learning, development, education and training

9 Kolb's experiential learning cycle

There are five essential dimensions of effective learning design: general rules governing the development, organization and presentation of learning:

1 It needs to be learner centred.

2 It needs to be a managed programme.

3 It needs to be an effective learning experience.

4 It needs to be a learning process, not just the provision of information.

5 It needs to use all available resources to enhance learning.

1 *Learner centred*. Learning design should begin with the learners – their needs and their point of view. The designer should try to think like a learner, and understand how learners will approach the learning. The learning design needs to engage the learner and provide a regular stimulus to maintain interest and the desire to continue. It should give clear direction to the learner, but allow scope for individual variation and for personalizing the learning.

2 *A managed programme*. In order to transfer learning to the workplace and achieve measurable business outcomes, a disciplined framework is needed. This should include clear aims and objectives, a system of quality assurance, a plan for evaluation and a focus on results. This means managing the integral or internal programme processes – ensuring learner completions, compliance with deadlines, achievement of outcomes, system efficiencies and so on – and it also means ensuring the external validity of the course, managing its transfer and application, and its impact on real business outcomes. The design must allow learners to achieve all their outcomes, and the business to achieve all of its results. Without a managed programme, there is chaos; with a managed programme, everything else starts to fall into place.

3 *An effective learning experience.* Designing a course is not the same thing as designing a learning experience. Experiential learning requires that people learn through what they do and what they discover for themselves. It is possible to plan how these acts and discoveries will happen, and thus direct learning towards planned outcomes, but it needs to be something the learners undertake for themselves. In other words, again, it needs to be learner centred. It needs to offer an active, not a passive, learning experience, which means learners become engaged, think through issues and solve problems. There needs to be plenty of scope for interactivity: with resources, among learners, and with people in support roles, including managers, mentors and tutors. It needs to include ways to engage different parts of the brain. It needs to make sure, wherever possible, that it's a memorable learning experience and that it's fun. And it needs to take account of different learning style preferences.

4 *A learning process.* When designing learning, there often needs to be more focus on the learning process than the content. This means creating a learning structure, whereby the learner has a navigational guide through the learning. There should be a clear path for the learner to follow, with extra readings, assessments or other resources and activities offered as bonuses to the main journey. Learners should never be expected to work their way through screeds of reading material as the main function of the course or programme. Rather, readings should augment the way learning is provided. This is not to say reading is not an important part of learning – of course it is, and people should be encouraged to read – but they need to choose how and when they read, and we need to recognize that large volumes of reading material are off-putting and can confuse key messages.

5 *Using resources to enhance learning.* It seems obvious to say that effective design should involve using resources to enable learning and to enhance the learning experience, yet this fundamental point is often overlooked. Sometimes, especially with new resources such as the latest digital technology, they can become the focus, rather than the learning itself, and this is especially true when people are dazzled by gadgetry just because it is impressive in itself – the 'gee whiz factor'. The trick is to look for ways the resources can make the learning experience better. This is the deciding factor – whether they can make the learning work better. If they can't, then no matter how

smart or expensive the resources may be they are just not appropriate. Good resources can transform an ordinary learning experience into something extraordinary, but bad or inappropriate resources often simply help to highlight poor learning design. Managers need to be prudent in choosing resources that actually help, not hinder, what they're trying to accomplish. The internet offers some of the richest media resources available today; it offers dynamic content such as video, audio and animation, great communication potential for both synchronous and asynchronous learning, and an ideal opportunity to coordinate and direct offline activities. These resources can make a great impact and a real difference to learning.

FURTHER READING

Bray, T (2009) *The Training Design Manual: The complete practical guide to creating effective and successful training programmes*, Kogan Page, London

Fee, K (2009) *Delivering E-Learning*, Kogan Page, London

Kalantzis, M, Cope, B and the Learning by Design Project Group (2005) *Learning By Design*, Common Ground, Melbourne

Piskurich, G, Beckschi, P and Hall, B (eds) (1999) *The ASTD Handbook of Training Design and Delivery: A comprehensive guide to creating and delivering training programs – instructor-led, computer-based or self-directed*, McGraw-Hill, New York

41 The route map model for e-learning design

X-REF TOOLS

38 The three component parts of e-learning

39 The five models of e-learning

40 Learning design: the five dimensions

Tool 40 looked at design of learning in general; this tool is about applying those principles to the specific circumstances of e-learning.

When designing an e-learning course, it can help to think of it as a journey, to be taken by the learners, and to offer the learners a route map to guide them on that journey. As they progress through a series of e-learning screens, they should be following the road signs that show them each step along the way, and the final destination at the end of the route.

The key idea of the route map in Figure 2.4 is to separate the signposting of the route to be followed from the branches off the main route – the side streets, lay-bys and loops that include the detailed content learners have to absorb, and that offer opportunities for them to test and discuss ideas. Thus the branches include: readings (usually PDFs or Word documents, or similar, unless they are very small); resources such as presentations, simulations, sound clips and videos (anything mainly passive, just like readings); activities such as discussions, games, simulations (the ones that require more active learner input, rather than just observation) and practical exercises (anything mainly active, requiring a high degree of learner input); and assessments (of both formative and summative types, and of all formats).

FIGURE 2.4 The route map model for e-learning design

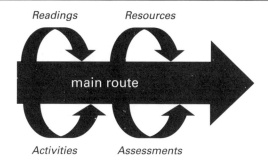

All of the branches ultimately converge, and so there should be more than one way of arriving at the destination, the end of the course. There will be many distractions along the branches, but the final destination will always be clear. Along the main route, the pages will be deliberately sparse, including essentially signposting – headings, aims, instructions, key points, and illustrations of these – but nothing else. The bulk of the course content will lie in the branches.

This is not the only formula for e-learning design, but it is one that has proved very successful, and an antidote to many of the duller implementations around, especially passive examples of 'e-reading'.

FURTHER READING

Chapnick, S and Meloy, J (2005) *Renaissance eLearning*, Wiley, San Francisco

Fee, K (2009) *Delivering E-Learning*, Kogan Page, London

Hussain, S (2005) *Developing E-Learning Materials: Applying user-centred design*, National Institute of Adult Continuing Education, Leicester

42 A classification of e-learning technologies

X-REF TOOLS

38 The three component parts of e-learning

39 The five models of e-learning

43 What to look for in a digital learning platform

44 Checklist – 10 things to look out for when dealing with e-learning vendors

E-learning technologies may be classified into the following five categories:

1 virtual learning environments (VLEs);

2 authoring tools;

3 collaborative tools;

4 assessment tools;

5 specialist software.

1 *Virtual learning environments (VLEs)*. A VLE is a platform for managing and delivering learning. A 'platform' is a generic term for a software framework, including system architecture, operating systems and programming languages. VLEs are platforms specifically adapted for learning. VLEs sometimes go by other names, such as managed learning environments, but some other terms that are used for them actually have more specific meanings, including learner management system, learning content management system, and virtual classroom. A learner management system (LMS) is a system for manipulating information about learners. A learning content management system (LCMS) is a system for organizing the learning – a repository for storing, retrieving and launching courses or their components. A virtual classroom is a means of staging learning

events for participants in different locations. VLEs can also include some of the technologies classified under the remaining headings.

2 *Authoring tools.* Anyone who is familiar with a computer programming language can use it to create web pages and anything on them: authoring tools enable anyone who doesn't have programming skills to do the same. In e-learning, authoring tools enable users to create learning content from scratch, typically in a simple template where authors can view the output, while they input it, exactly as it will appear to learners. Authoring tools often enable authors to create 'learning objects', which may be stored, retrieved and reused in other courses or aggregates of learning content.

3 *Collaborative tools.* Collaborative tools enable learners to interact with other learners and work together on issues of common interest. Examples include wikis, blogs, discussion forums, live chat and virtual classrooms. Wikis are web pages where learners can share the development of content and discuss its progress. Blogs are like online diaries, or logs, where the blogger writes and publishes his or her thoughts, and subscribers to the blog can post comments or questions. Discussion forums allow multiple users to start discussion topics, or threads, and reply to threads started by others; this allows learners to hold multi-sided online discussions about topics of common interest. Live chat is a synchronized version of a discussion forum, where contributors agree to meet and chat at a set time. Virtual classrooms are web-based meetings organized as lessons or tutorials, where the participants have audio and perhaps video contact, a shared whiteboard, and access to shared documents.

4 *Assessment tools.* Assessment technologies range from simple tools for setting and marking quizzes to more complex software for analysing the style of a piece of writing. They are especially good at handling objective testing methods like multiple choice questions, true/false questions and hotspot questions (where the learner has to select an area of a diagram, map or illustration). They are limited in their ability to assess free text answers, such as essays, owing to the vast and complex range of possible answers.

5 *Specialist software.* This fifth category is a catch-all for technologies that don't quite fit in the other four categories, and as such it is always expanding. It includes simulations, games, study and revision tools, three-dimensional panoramic imaging software, and virtual characters, or avatars – and anything else that enhances the e-learning experience.

FURTHER READING

A slightly adapted version of this tool originally appeared in Fee, K (2009) *Delivering E-Learning*, Kogan Page, London

43 What to look for in a digital learning platform

Digital learning platforms are the enabling software that allow the applications of leading-edge technologies to learning and development solutions. With a good platform, an organization may implement a much wider range of e-learning and blended learning opportunities than it previously could, and offer more powerful learning solutions.

These platforms are known by a number of names, perhaps most commonly virtual learning environments or VLEs, but also managed learning environments or managed learning systems. Some other terms that are used for them actually have more specific meanings: a VLE can include a learner management system, a learning content management system, and a virtual classroom, plus other, ancillary functions.

A learner management system, or LMS, is a means of manipulating information about learners. By building a database of learners, an organization can track their progress as they go through courses, and can generate reports classified in many ways, such as by learning route, occupation, location, gender, age profile, etc. The bigger the organization, the more useful this information can be. The drawbacks to an LMS are that its benefits really depend on economies of scale (so it's of limited value to a small business or any relatively small learning community) and the information in its reports tends to comprise metrics about 'housekeeping' rather than performance improvement – it can tell a lot about how well it works within its own parameters, but not so much about how it adds value to the organization.

A learning content management system, or LCMS, is a means of organizing the learning – a repository for storing, retrieving and launching courses or their components. This can generate reports too, such as uptake of courses, success rates, etc, but the real benefits are in managing the learning content, and so an LCMS should be used in tandem with an authoring tool – indeed many include an authoring tool. This combination enables the user to write and store courses, and their building blocks, reusable learning objects. The main drawback of an LCMS is its focus on 'content' rather than learning experiences; it is really just a slightly specialized version of a generic software application, the content management system, used in various information processing contexts.

A virtual classroom is a means of staging learning events for participants in different locations. The virtual classroom is a development from the technology for videoconferencing and online meetings, to enable online lectures, seminars, tutorials and discussion workshops – all kinds of live e-learning. It works by using webcams and screens (for visual contact), microphones and speakers or headsets (for audio contact), shared screen space to take the place of the chalkboard, flipchart or slide projector, and shared access to documents. The virtual classroom is a good example of technology for a *synchronous* e-learning experience, one where learners 'get together' (in their various locations) at the same times, as distinct from an *asynchronous* e-learning experience, where learners can undertake the same e-learning at different times and at their own pace.

The following factors should be weighed when choosing a platform:

- *Learning needs*. An organization looking to introduce a digital learning platform needs, first, to know what it needs and, secondly, to consider the above capabilities and decide which of them best meet those needs.

- *Costs*. Some platforms are very expensive to implement, running to tens of thousands of pounds, if not into six figures, and yet there are open source software and freeware versions available that avoid these costs altogether. The world market-leading digital platform, Moodle, is an example of the open source approach, ably demonstrating that there is no need to pay for a platform at all. Of course, there are still costs in implementing any sort of platform, but paying for a proprietary product's development investment is not necessary.

- *Interoperability*. The buyer or acquirer needs to be confident that the content put into the platform can be retrieved and reused in another context, perhaps on another platform. SCORM standard compliance is the shorthand way of dealing with this; simple back-up procedures are another safeguard; but the platform itself should be interrogated for what it offers to ensure or facilitate interoperability.

- *Additional functions.* Lastly, a great benefit of any platform will be its capacity to add on further software tools to offer additional functionality. It can be hard to spot this sort of flexibility in advance, but worth testing whenever the opportunity arises, as this may be a key factor in keeping the platform useful for the future.

FURTHER READING

Fee, K (2009) *Delivering E-Learning*, Kogan Page, London
http://moodle.org/
http://www.learningcircuits.org

Checklist – 10 things to look out for when dealing with e-learning vendors

44

X-REF TOOLS

38 The three component parts of e-learning

39 The five models of e-learning

42 A classification of e-learning technologies

45 What to look for in a learning and development consultant

In my previous book, *Delivering E-Learning*, I took a sceptical view of e-learning vendors, highlighting their shortcomings and warning against some of their misleading positions. I don't believe vendors of e-learning products and services, as distinct from vendors of other learning and development services, are especially cynical or dishonest; I'm sure their motives and behaviour are every bit as reputable. However, e-learning is a field in which HR and IT collide, and both disciplines claim a greater understanding. I contend that this causes problems, especially where technological considerations override the primacy of the learner's needs.

Therefore, those who purchase e-learning products and services need to be especially on their guard. In *Delivering E-Learning*, I identified 20 'things to be wary of with vendors'. Here, I suggest a more manageable list of 10 potential problems areas, selected on the basis that they may be the more problematic areas, and because they may have wider applicability to other learning and development service vendors:

1. E-learning vendors have encouraged the view that e-learning is completely different from learning – the truth is that it's just the application of digital technology to some aspects of learning and development, and is therefore a subset of general learning and development.

2. The way vendors define e-learning is often misleading because their definitions are devised to lend disproportionate importance to their own offers. They present the world with themselves at its centre. The antidote to this is that buyers need to develop a clear perspective of how e-learning fits in their context, and therefore a sense of proportion as to what the vendor may contribute.

3. Vendors frequently use technological jargon to mystify e-learning, when they should be trying to make it more accessible. HR professionals can be equally guilty of this, but that doesn't excuse the techies. The way to combat this is by 'playing daft' and asking for the meaning of the first obscure or esoteric term offered.

4. Vendors rarely know much about learning, yet usually profess to be experts in e-learning – you can't be one without the other. A vendor's simplistic understanding of learning can lead to technology of limited value, missed opportunities, and poor e-learning implementations. Buyers need to have their own clear vision of what their learning is aiming to accomplish, and lock the vendor into that.

5. Vendors often claim to offer complete e-learning solutions, when in fact their core competence lies in just one part of the solution. See tool 42 for clarification of this, and be ready to challenge exaggerated claims.

6. The benefits vendors claim for e-learning serve more to make the vendor's business case than to identify real benefits for their clients. One common example is that 'scalability' helps vendors target larger clients, but is meaningless for small to medium-sized clients, or those looking for small-scale implementations. Buyers need to ensure that the focus is on their specific challenges, and dismiss anything else as irrelevant.

7. Vendors typically just sell their products, rather than helping identify clients' problems and finding solutions for them. This is certainly a more common issue than just in the market for e-learning; vendors should be encouraged to take a more consultative approach, and be dropped if they are unwilling or unable to comply.

8. Vendors often propose unique approaches to the development and implementation of e-learning, when learning and development professionals already have planning models that will work just as well for e-learning.

9 Vendors overemphasize the importance of e-learning technology standards. This relates to point 3 above. As digital technologies become more and more commoditized, standards become less relevant; interoperability is important, but standards are not a 'magic bullet', and vendors need to be led to the goal of interoperability, not permitted to sidetrack the debate into the often irrelevant jargon of standards.

10 Vendors sometimes offer misleading price information, excluding items such as updates or expenses, which can be a high proportion of the client's real costs. This is a much broader concern than just with e-learning, and may be tackled in part by testing and exploring the limits of applicability of each service, and its related costs. But, ultimately, a vendor who repeatedly misleads is not playing fair, and deserves to be dropped.

FURTHER READING

Fee, K (2009) *Delivering E-Learning*, Kogan Page, London

45 What to look for in a learning and development consultant

X-REF TOOLS

35 A checklist for procuring learning services

36 Outsourcing versus insourcing

44 Checklist – 10 things to look out for when dealing with e-learning vendors

88 How to get value from learning consultants

There are all sorts of learning and development consultants in the market. Some are independent individuals, others are small groups of associates, and still more are big international firms with substantial resources. Their services vary enormously, and their prices do too. This presents a challenge to any organization looking to retain consultants. This tool offers two processes, the first a simple format for measuring a consultant's fit, the second a more detailed checklist.

To begin with the first process, consultants may be measured against three criteria already very familiar to anyone involved in learning and development:

- *Knowledge.* Do the consultants have expertise in the prospective client's business, specific know-how in the subject(s) or discipline(s) under consideration, or industry or sector knowledge such as knowledge of relevant occupational standards? Do they have knowledge of the consultancy process, and the processes they may have to apply in the course of their engagement?

- *Skills*. Do the consultants have the following skills: listening, interviewing, presentation, facilitation, problem solving, project management, report writing, or any other skills that may be identified in advance as crucial to the process?

- *Attitude*. Are the consultants independent self-starters? Are they confident and assertive, but at the same time open-minded, flexible and responsive to new information and ideas? Do they have a good customer focus and a healthy respect for the client's needs and culture?

Having established these basics, here is the checklist. Consultants may be measured against the following key criteria:

1 *Test consultants' credibility*. This may be established from: client testimonials; the consultants' personal credentials, such as qualifications or experience; the professionalism shown in the way they conduct themselves and in things like the quality of their marketing materials.

2 *Look for evidence of relevant skills*. This may be established from the pre-contract selection process, in which the consultants may demonstrate any of the skills detailed above, and perhaps many more.

3 *Look for evidence of preparation*. Have the consultants done their homework on the client organization? This could be a good indicator of how thorough they will be in carrying out subsequent work.

4 *Look for evidence of availability*. Do they have the scope to dedicate sufficient time and attention to the project, or do they seem heavily committed elsewhere?

5 *Look for evidence of financial viability*. How long have the consultants been in business? (A typical measure is to check whether they can show accounts for the past three years.) Do they have the financial resources to meet their ongoing running costs and service the client's project? How big a proportion of their turnover is the project?

6 *Check affordability*. Are the consultants' fees within the client's budget, and what value can they return?

7 *Consider back-up*. If the client contracts with an individual consultant, what happens if the consultant falls sick or is otherwise unable to complete the project within the agreed timescale? Does the consultant have colleagues or associates?

8 *Ask for insurance*. Professional indemnity insurance may not seem necessary for most learning and development work, but it is

inexpensive and easy to obtain, which raises the question why some consultants don't have it.

9 *Consider responsiveness and flexibility.* Are the consultants prompt to recognize the client's needs and respond to them? Are they able to change and adapt as circumstances change?

10 *Don't forget personal and cultural fit.* Will the consultants be sympathetic to the client organization's culture, and readily adjust themselves to the people they meet?

FURTHER READING

Bailey, D and Sproston, C (1993) *Choosing and Using Training Consultants*, Gower, Aldershot

Lewis, H (2006) *Choosing and Using Consultants and Advisers: A best practice guide to making the right decision and getting good value*, Kogan Page, London

http://www.mdn.org.uk/choosing.htm (accessed November 2010)

What to look for in learning materials

46

X-REF TOOL

79 Checklist for setting up a learning centre

This tool comprises a suite of questions to ask when considering the suitability of any learner resource. The resource could be a training manual, an online course, a video-based resource, a workbook or other published learning materials, or any other resource for learners; regardless of what it comprises, it may be interrogated using the following classified list of questions. There are 20 questions, subdivided into five clusters of four:

Content:

1 Is it pitched at the right level to meet learner needs?

2 Does it offer sufficient breadth of coverage?

3 Is there enough depth (or, conversely, too much detail)?

4 Are the objectives viable and appropriate?

Structure and relevance:

5 Is the structure logical and coherent?

6 Are units in manageable sections (too long, too short)?

7 Is the content up to date, and will it remain so?

8 Is it consistent with other material used by the organization?

Format and media:

9 Are the selected media accessible and do they meet learner needs?

10 Are the media fit for purpose?

11 Is the format tried and tested?

12 Do the media and format match organizational requirements?

Learning design issues:

13 Does the material include features that will actually help learners to learn?

14 Are there regular opportunities for self-assessment and feedback?

15 Does the material link easily to any accreditation?

16 Does the material lend itself readily to evaluation?

Style and presentation:

17 Does the presentation contribute to the material's effectiveness?

18 Does the style fit with the organization's style?

19 Does the style limit its use to certain groups?

20 Do learners actually like it?

This is not a definitive list of questions, and others may be added, but the manager should beware of asking too many questions, as there comes a point when the questioning has to stop and a decision has to be made, on the basis of the evidence available from the questions used thus far. When to stop questioning, and when to move to a decision, is a matter for judgement.

When comparing a number of competing resources to address a particular need, a matrix may be constructed by ranging the questions along one axis, and the contending resources along the other axis. This allows ease of comparison and, by weighting the responses (eg one point for a qualified yes, two points for a definitive yes), scores may be added and compared to introduce greater objectivity into the selection decision.

FURTHER READING

Rowntree, D (1997) *Making Materials-Based Learning Work*, Routledge, London

Working with union learning representatives

47

> **X-REF TOOLS**
>
> **14** How to develop a learning culture
> **15** How to develop a learning organization
> **26** Board-level development: a needs audit

A long with tool 26, this is one of just two tools in this book that will not be, at least in theory, applicable to everyone. Working with union learning representatives will only be relevant to organizations where there is a trade union presence or there is likely to be one in the near future. Nevertheless, this tool may be of useful reference to others.

Trade union learning representatives are the linchpin of an initiative called Unionlearn, which was launched by the Trades Union Congress (TUC) in 2006, with funding of £4.5 million from the Department for Education and Skills in England and Wales, and 120 dedicated staff. Unionlearn has become a recognized brand for TUC-sponsored courses and learning centres in colleges, union offices and workplaces throughout the UK.

Unionlearn promotes lifelong learning and has three aims:

1 to help unions to become learning organizations, with programmes for union representatives and regional officers, and strategic support for national officers;

2 to help unions to broker learning opportunities for their members, running phone and online advice services, securing the best courses to meet learners' needs and kitemarking union academy provision to a quality standard;

3 to research union priorities on learning and skills, identify and share good practice, promote learning agreements, support union members on learning and skills bodies, and help shape sector skills agreements.

The range of provision addressed by Unionlearn includes adult literacy and numeracy, and basic skills to make union members more competitive in the job market and their career development. Unionlearn has targeted areas where learning opportunities may not otherwise be available, and has a special focus on helping low-paid, low-skilled workers, who are often among those least able to engage with learning.

The union learning representatives are spread across every workplace where there is union representation, and aim to encourage learning from a perspective other than the directives of employers. Such a role may be superfluous in many cases, but in some it could provide a fresh insight and perspective, and draw into learning some who might otherwise miss out. This may be the difference that could be injected even into organizations where there is no trade union; staff representatives, or perhaps other stakeholders from family, customers, suppliers, shareholders or the local community, could provide the catalyst to help get more employees into learning.

Illustrative example

Jimmy Willis, a union learning representative with First Bus, based in Glasgow, undertook to learn Polish, in order to help migrant worker colleagues settle in. Taking this a natural step further, Willis moved on to teach bus drivers dialect expressions, colloquialisms, and quirks of the Glasgow accent, and to translate from the local idiom. This has helped Polish bus drivers better understand some of the more idiosyncratic – and less comprehensible – destination and fare requests of their passengers. For his distinctive approach, Willis earned a special award in 2009 from the Scottish TUC, and his story was featured on the BBC Scotland television news.

Over the last decade, the Union Learning Fund overseen by Unionlearn has disbursed over £100,000 of funding for learning, and a recent landmark was the celebration of having trained 22,000 union learning representatives. This is a large-scale initiative with implications that are increasingly difficult to afford to ignore.

FURTHER READING

Shelley, S and Calveley, M (2007) *Learning with Trade Unions: A contemporary agenda in employment relations*, Ashgate, Aldershot
http://www.unionlearn.org.uk/

Using qualifications

Qualifications in learning and development are primarily motivational tools. Because they reward the individual learner, because they are nationally or internationally recognized, and because they are portable and durable, they serve as robust, lasting testaments to the achievements and capabilities of learners.

Some organizations have been put off using qualifications for precisely these reasons, because they fear that the individuals in whom they have invested so heavily, paying their tuition fees, giving them paid time off work and so forth, may repay this investment by leaving to find another employer that will pay or otherwise reward them more, or offer them their next career challenge. This fear leads some employers to offer courses and other learning opportunities that deliberately do not include qualifications: these employers are missing the point.

In any survey of learners, there will always be those who do make a career move after obtaining a qualification, but many more will choose to stay with the employer that gave them the opportunity to learn and obtain that qualification. Recognizing that employees are increasingly mobile in the employment market, the employers of choice will be those that, among other things, give their employees opportunities to learn and develop. Offering qualifications may be one way of retaining employees for as long as possible.

Some may argue that the learning itself, and accomplishment of its goals, should be sufficient reward, but qualifications are the proof of that, and the transferable means whereby learners or employees can benchmark their achievements.

Qualifications are also tools for recording assessment and attainment, as in Kirkpatrick's second level of evaluation. Where we use qualifications for this purpose, and where the qualifications are sufficiently robust, we can be confident that we are generating good evidence of the success (or not) of learning.

Some qualifications are better than others. Some have tradable value, often based less on the qualification itself than on the reputation of the awarding institution. Some qualifications are more instantly recognizable – and therefore valuable – than others: compare, for example, an MBA with an NVQ in management. Competence- and work-based qualifications tend not to have the same appeal as more established, academic-style qualifications, but they have other advantages. They relate directly to what learners can do and have proved they can do, and they can easily be compared with other qualifications, to get a sense of the level learners can operate at.

Organizations need to exercise judgement: they need to choose qualifications that provide the evidence they are looking for, and at the same time offer enough incentive for the learners. It's a fine judgement, but getting the balance right can make a great difference to how well learning works.

FURTHER READING

Ecclestone, K (2005) *Understanding Assessment and Qualifications in Post-Compulsory Education and Training*, National Institute of Adult Continuing Education, Leicester

Kogan Page publishes an annual guide to professional, vocational and academic qualifications in the UK: *British Qualifications 2011: A complete guide to professional, vocational and academic qualifications in the UK*, Kogan Page, London, 2010

The Register of Regulated Qualifications contains details of recognized awarding organizations and regulated qualifications in England (Ofqual), Wales (DCELLS) and Northern Ireland (Ofqual for vocational qualifications and CCEA for all other qualifications): http://register.ofqual.gov.uk/

Reference list of learning and development methods

X-REF TOOLS

27 Learning methods and styles grid
28 Learning methods choice matrix
33 Using different approaches to learning and development
34 Criteria for choosing a learning approach

This tool offers a list to choose from when considering learning and development methods. As an inventory, it cannot hope to be exhaustive, but should provide a simple guide to most of the commonly recognized learning and development methods. Each method is listed, in alphabetical order, and followed by a brief description:

- *360-degree feedback*. This describes when performance and development review includes feedback from the learner's peers, colleagues and subordinates – everyone from a 360-degree range of the learner.
- *Accelerated learning*. A way of directing learning that aims to follow the way the brain naturally works, and thus to make learning faster and more efficient.
- *Action learning*. A group approach, developed by Reg Revans, whereby an action learning group or set analyses real work problems, develops solutions and acts upon them.
- *Benchmarking*. Identifying a model, or benchmark, elsewhere (perhaps in another organization), learning from it and seeking to emulate it.

- *Blended learning.* A combination of online learning with offline learning, often a misnomer for blended training, as it is the learners who do the blending.
- *Brainstorming.* The generation of ideas, by individuals or groups, in a non-evaluative way, to maximize the range of options for subsequent analysis.
- *Case studies.* The examination, by individuals or groups, of events or situations, usually from real life, analysis in some detail, and consideration of solutions to problems.
- *Coaching.* Usually a one-to-one process, whereby a more experienced senior colleague or external specialist gives guidance to the learner, typically with a focus on tasks or functions.
- *Conferences.* Large meeting events that may be attended and participated in as a means of personal or career development, or sometimes to allow a large group to consider a large, or multifaceted, developmental task.
- *Corporate universities.* Centrally organized learning and development provision, under a corporate brand.
- *Counselling.* Like coaching, except that the focus is on the person, not on tasks and functions, addressing concerns such as motivation or self-confidence.
- *Courses.* The most common off-the-job learning method, consisting of meetings of learners, with a teacher or trainer, in a classroom environment, following a syllabus.
- *Critical incident analysis.* This involves isolation of a critical incident from a more complex set of circumstances, for detailed analysis and discussion, and is founded on the assumption that the critical incident is the most important factor.
- *Demonstration.* This occurs where instruction is accompanied by showing the learner exactly what to do, such as how to manipulate tools or operate equipment.
- *Deputizing.* A designated deputy stands in for the usual role holder and gets a sustained opportunity to practise that role.
- *Development centres.* Concentrated multi-activity events, typically taking place over two to three days, including group work, interviews, exercises, psychometric tests and more, often for succession planning or similar.
- *Discovery learning.* An informal method of learning by doing, where learners discover for themselves what they need to know or how to do things.
- *Distance learning.* Where the learner and trainer are separated by distance and communicate using correspondence, telephone, e-mail and any other means for exchange of resources and learner support.

- *Drama-based learning.* The logical extension of role play, usually featuring scripted input and perhaps professional actors, to act out real-life situations.
- *e-learning.* The collective term for all forms of digitally resourced learning, including online courses, blended learning, live e-learning events such as webinars, use of online learning resources, and electronic performance support.
- *Encounter groups.* A specialized form of group work based on a confrontational approach, where participants are encouraged to say what they really feel, regardless of the consequences.
- *Executive coaching.* This usually refers to a combination of coaching and mentoring for senior managers.
- *Exhibitions.* An event featuring large numbers of organizations displaying goods and services, which may be attended as a vehicle for personal or career development.
- *Facilitation.* The means whereby learners are supported to learn, usually in an off-the-job context like a course or workshop.
- *Fishbowl exercise.* A group technique where one sub-group undertakes a task, while a second sub-group observes them, and then both sub-groups join together for feedback and shared learning.
- *Flexible learning.* A rather vague term for learning methods that allow learners flexibility to learn where, when and at the pace they choose; open and distance learning are examples of flexible learning.
- *Games.* Resources that encourage learning through game playing are usually deployed in coursework and e-learning; they benefit from being fun to play; and they may be computer based, board games, or the active play type.
- *Guided practice.* This is where learners are supported in actually doing a job or task, with guidance on where they go wrong as well as where they get it right.
- *Guided reading.* Reading is one of the best ways of acquiring knowledge; guided reading is a proactive way of directing study, perhaps augmented by group support and discussion.
- *Instruction.* One of the simplest learning methods, when learners are given written or verbal direction on how to undertake a task or function; instruction can take place on the job or off the job.
- *In-tray or inbox exercise.* An old-fashioned simulation of a real in-tray or inbox, containing a number of items of administration requiring the learner's attention; this addresses issues like decision making, problem solving, prioritizing, time management and attention to detail.

- *Job rotation.* When an employee is moved from one job role to another ('rotated' through two or more roles) to obtain a fresh perspective (see *Secondment*).

- *Lateral thinking.* A term devised by Edward de Bono to describe looking at a problem or a situation in an unorthodox or unconventional way – thinking laterally.

- *Learning centre.* The provision of facilities to make available learning resources, study space and a focus for learning. Also known as a learning resource centre.

- *Learning contract.* A document recording learning that it is agreed will take place, signed off by all the participants, eg the learner, the learner's manager, the trainer, etc. The idea is that this promotes commitment to the learning.

- *Learning log/journal/diary.* Maintenance of a precise written record of learning as it takes place, with a view to reinforcing that learning.

- *Lecture.* The most traditional, and most didactic, teaching method on a course, in which a lengthy presentation is delivered, usually supported by audio-visual aids, and followed by questions and perhaps some discussion.

- *Mentoring.* Like coaching, but goes beyond tasks or functions to focus on the learner's capability, potential and career-related personal development.

- *Mind mapping.* Devised by Tony Buzan, this involves writing down all the ideas associated with a concept, in the form of a diagram (or mind map) with linking lines showing the relationships between different parts. This is probably more useful as an individual rather than a group method.

- *Networking.* Essentially about keeping in touch with other people, as a development technique this is about using a wide network of contacts to gain different insights or specific knowledge. Increasingly popular online.

- *Online learning.* The use of courses or learning resources on the world wide web, or on a corporate intranet or network. The most common form of e-learning.

- *Open learning.* Widely confused with distance and flexible learning, the 'open' aspect is about opening access to learning, by removing barriers of time (as in flexible learning), barriers of distance (as in distance learning) or entry requirements (as in higher education). Pioneered in the UK by the Open University, and still popular, although eclipsed to some extent by e-learning.

- *Outdoor development.* This method uses the outdoor environment, and activities like orienteering, camping, climbing and sailing (and associated equipment) to develop personal attributes, to promote teamwork and to encourage learners to think differently about tasks and their roles. This is often called 'Outward Bound', but this is a brand name.

- *Panel discussion*. Where a group of experts discuss issues for the benefit of an audience of learners, who may then ask questions and broaden the discussion, in the style of the long-running BBC television programme *Question Time*.

- *Performance and development review*. This is sometimes called appraisal or performance review, but at the expense of ignoring the developmental aspect, which is about regular meetings between the learner and his or her manager to consider the learner's work performance and how it can be improved, with the accent on learning and development. This is often linked to a personal development plan.

- *Personal development plan*. Individual records that map out the direction an individual's development will take. Also known as learning plans, or just action plans.

- *Portfolio*. A highly structured learning log, based on certain pro-forma documents, with supporting evidence of the learner's experience. May be either digital or paper based. Used extensively in the UK for National Vocational Qualifications (NVQs).

- *Psychometric instruments*. Often used for selection and assessment, these can also be developmental tools, if used in the right way, with the emphasis on the outcomes of tests or candidate profiles. These can be used as a basis for discussion, to promote self-awareness, tease out development needs, and encourage individuals to review their own learning.

- *Reading*. Self-explanatory. One of the simplest ways of absorbing new information and acquiring knowledge.

- *Resource-based learning*. Providing resources to help learners learn, including books, CDs, DVDs and online resources. This method includes promotion of private study and research, and the organization of learning through resource centres.

- *Role play*. Acting parts in an artificial scenario where two or more learners take on the roles, perhaps to enact a problem situation at work, in order to reach a resolution.

- *Secondment*. When an employee is moved, or seconded, to another role for a set period of time. A secondment may be within an organization, perhaps in another region or country, or more commonly with a separate organization.

- *Seminars*. More interactive than a lecture, a seminar is a learning method for a small tutorial group, which may involve some lecturing, but more facilitation of group discussion.

- *Shadowing.* When the learner works alongside someone else – shadowing the person's role – in order to learn from that person (see *Sitting-by-Nellie*).

- *Sitting-by-Nellie.* The colloquial expression, widely used, for learning by working alongside an experienced practitioner, as with a skilled worker and an apprentice.

- *Sponsoring.* This method involves a senior colleague adopting the learner and assisting the learner's development and career progression.

- *Storytelling.* This method draws on the belief that people absorb information better in the form of an anecdote or a tale. Thus the idea is to incorporate storytelling into coursework or to elicit stories from learners.

- *Structured debate.* A group discussion circumscribed by a set of rules, such as parliamentary procedure, in order to provide better focus for the discussion.

- *Syndicates.* Also known as breakout groups, syndicates are small learning groups formed when a larger group is subdivided to allow greater specialization in discussion, or to allow different syndicates to tackle separate issues before reporting back to a plenary session.

- *Teaching.* One of the most powerful learning techniques is when a learner is required to teach a subject, and thus obtain not just a fresh perspective, but a deeper insight into it.

- *Team building.* A work-based learning method for encouraging cooperation, sharing of information, and mutual credit for work well done. The metaphor, drawn from the world of sports and games, is that group work is more cohesive and effective when members work together as a team.

- *Video.* Like reading, watching videos, films or movies is one of the simplest ways of absorbing new information and acquiring knowledge.

- *Virtual learning centre.* The digital equivalent of a learning centre, with a range of resources held electronically and accessed online or via a corporate network.

- *Volunteering-based learning.* An opportunity to practise and demonstrate knowledge and skills in a voluntary context.

- *Work-based project.* A prescribed and distinct piece of work, which may be undertaken by an individual or a group as a learning exercise (as well as any immediate work benefit), incorporating planning and reporting, among other skills. Also known as a work-based assignment.

- *Workshop.* A small group tutorial with the emphasis on practical activities.

FURTHER READING

Clark, R C (2010) *Evidence-Based Training Methods: A guide for training professionals*, ASTD Press, Alexandria, VA
Hart, L (1991) *Training Methods that Work: A handbook for trainers*, Crisp Publications, Menlo Park, CA
Pike, R (1994) *Creative Training Techniques Handbook: Tips, tactics and how-to's for delivering effective training*, Jossey-Bass, San Francisco
http://en.wikipedia.org/wiki/Category:Learning_methods
http://www.cipd.co.uk/subjects/lrnanddev/designdelivery/creatmthds.htm (accessed November 2010)

PART THREE
Implementing learning

This part of the book considers a range of 30 tools that contribute to implementing learning.

Icebreakers

In any situation where people meet each other for the first time, or after not having met for a while, there is an atmosphere of some tension or discomfort. Some people are shy, some express their discomfort through abrasiveness, or aloofness, or by being withdrawn, and most people are uncertain how to interact with others in this sort of situation. This undermines learning: for learning to flourish people need to be at their ease, and there needs to be a climate of openness and trust.

Therefore something needs to be done to dissolve the inhibiting atmosphere and encourage shared feelings of positivity among the group. The metaphor is that the waters that make up the gathering are frozen, and something needs to be done to help them to thaw and melt, but we don't have a lot of time, so we need to break the ice.

'Icebreakers' is the collective term for exercises used to introduce people meeting in a learning event. Icebreakers can also be useful in online learning situations, where the learners are meeting in some sort of virtual environment, and these will require to be slightly different, to accommodate this different context. When we discuss this tool we are mainly concerned with the face-to-face context.

The books and websites for 'Further reading' below give lots of generic examples that may be used as they are or may be adapted to the specific needs of a particular audience. Adaptation can be important, to ensure, for example, that nobody considers the icebreaker patronizing or too trivial. And care must be taken with a group who already know one another to break the ice in a way that does not unnecessarily reintroduce them.

Humour can be very important. It lightens the mood, and helps relax people, before getting down to the more serious business. Another good ploy, if feasible, is to try to link the icebreaker thematically to the subject of the learning event: a session on change management or evaluation can be opened with an icebreaker asking the learners to recount an instance when they have changed their mind about something – and why they did so.

Illustrative example

One icebreaker I have used myself recently is to invite the learners to introduce themselves (just their name and which organization or department they are from) and then tell the group two 'facts' about themselves – one a true fact and the other something they have made up. The others then need to guess which of the two 'facts' is true. This works because it can be a fun game, and it encourages people to open up and reveal a little about themselves, though the facilitator has to stand ready to reveal something about him- or herself first! I find this works best if the learners offer up their facts in the order they wish – volunteers first – rather than going round the room in the 'creeping death'.

FURTHER READING

Evans, A and Tizard, P (2003) *The Icebreakers Pocketbook*, Management Pocketbooks, Alresford

Newstrom, J and Scannell, E (2007) *The Big Book of Business Games: Icebreakers, creativity exercises, and meeting energizers*, McGraw-Hill, New York

http://insight.typepad.co.uk/40_icebreakers_for_small_groups.pdf (accessed December 2010)

http://www.icebreakers.ws/ (accessed December 2010)

Coaching – tips and pitfalls

X-REF TOOLS

49 Reference list of learning and development methods

54 How to mentor someone

56 Guided practice

73 Guided reading

Coaching is a powerful learning method, perhaps the foremost of David Clutterbuck's 'learning alliances'. Much has been written about coaching, and this book is not the place to attempt to distil the method, but a practical aid is to have a core list of some of the best tips to make use of and some of the worst pitfalls to avoid.

The top five tips are:

1 *Seize the opportunity to coach.* All of us have busy working lives, and it's not always easy to put aside time for coaching, but one of the worst things we can do is pass up a chance to help someone benefit from an experience with a keenly judged word here or there. One of the most important skills in coaching is spotting the opportunities.

2 *Use questions prudently.* Coaches should keep asking to probe a topic until they are sure they understand the issues; they should ask enough questions (although not too many), and try to ask the right questions. They should refine their questioning to get to the heart of the matter. The 5WH model is especially useful (who, what, where, when, why and how, especially 'why') to test understanding of everything.

3 *Use silences.* Nobody likes silences, and often the coach has to overcome the urge to fill them, giving the learner the opportunity to come in, in his or her own time. The coach should play the waiting game, and allow the learner time to gather his or her thoughts and open up.

4 *Listen effectively.* The coach should try to tune into what is important to the learner. The coach should look to pick up nuances, inferences and clues that the learner wants to divulge more, given a sympathetic ear.

5 *Translate into action.* The coach should be on the constant alert for converting ideas and opinions from the learner into a plan for action. This does not mean that the coach should form that plan, but rather that he or she should highlight the potential for transfer to the learner, and steer the learner towards formulating his or her own plan.

The worst five pitfalls are:

1 Missing informal coaching opportunities, or thinking about only formal coaching sessions and undervaluing the informal. 'Watercooler moments' or chance meetings in corridors can be among the most powerful coaching interventions.

2 Leaping to conclusions and solutions without taking enough time to gather information and consider all the different dimensions of a problem, and the points of view of everyone involved. Patience should be the watchword, and the coach should guard against impetuosity.

3 Talking too much. As a general rule, the learner should do a lot more talking than the coach.

4 Being too directive. Coaching is about guiding, not instructing. The coach shouldn't tell the learner the answer, but should let the learner find it for him- or herself.

5 Thinking that coaching is appropriate for every occasion – it's not.

FURTHER READING

Clutterbuck, D (1998) *Learning Alliances*, CIPD, London

Lee, G (2003) *Leadership Coaching: From personal insight to organisational performance*, CIPD, London

McMahon, G and Archer, A (eds) (2010) *101 Coaching Strategies and Techniques*, Routledge, London

Starr, J (2010) *The Coaching Manual: The definitive guide to the process, principles and skills of personal coaching*, Prentice Hall, Harlow

Whitmore, J (2009) *Coaching for Performance: Growing human potential and purpose – the principles and practice of coaching and leadership*, Nicholas Brealey, London

Facilitation – tips and pitfalls

52

X-REF TOOL

49 Reference list of learning and development methods

One of the biggest myths about learning and development is that it is about imparting information, and that the trainer must be a subject expert or a fount of knowledge. In fact, often the key role of the learning and development professional is to draw upon the experiences of learners and encourage them to use those experiences and share them with others. As with coaching, much has been written about facilitation, and this book is not the place to attempt to distil the method, but a practical aid is to have a core list of some of the best tips to make use of and some of the worst pitfalls to avoid.

The top five tips are:

1 Give learners more responsibility, including tasks often taken by the facilitator, such as scribing, or even facilitating a session. This is the clearest way of demonstrating that learning is their responsibility.

2 Variety is the spice of learning. Make sure each session is different from those that come before and after it, mixing up syndicate groups' numbers and personnel, moving people around, and varying the discussions, exercises and activities.

3 Treat learners with respect. Always remember that they are adults with considerable work experience and expertise in their jobs, and make sure that you show that to them in the way you behave towards them. Make them feel valued members of the group, with something to contribute.

4 Consider the group dynamic, and continuously review it. Make sure the sessions are working and that people are learning – and, if not, be ready to change things.

5 Keep it real. Be authentic as a facilitator and as a person. And keep checking everything is relevant to the learners and their work situation, as this ensures learning stays on track.

The worst five pitfalls are:

1 Don't be didactic. One of the worst things a facilitator can do is switch into lecturing mode and simply talk at the learners.

2 Never ignore a contribution because it is not immediately understood. When a learner says something that takes the facilitator by surprise, the temptation can be to ignore it, as it is hard to tell where it may lead. There is a risk that it could be irrelevant, and yet sometimes this sort of contribution can enrich the learning experience for everyone – including the facilitator.

3 Don't persist with things that aren't working. Facilitators, as the creators of the learning experience, run the risk of being too loyal to processes they believe in; the real test is whether they work for the learners, and if they don't they should be dropped, so that everyone can move on to something of more value.

4 Don't let things get out of control. Flexibility is fine, and some freewheeling is to be encouraged, but part of the facilitator's role is to regularly steer things back on track and to bear in mind the purpose and objectives. Don't mistake flexibility for lack of structure – the facilitator should maintain the integrity of the learning event.

5 Never allow problem behaviour by individuals, such as anger or disruptive actions, to spoil the experience for the group. Nip inappropriate behaviour in the bud. Be tolerant and open to people's feelings, but don't allow hostility or negativity to fester.

FURTHER READING

Bowman, S (2009) *Training from the Back of the Room! 65 ways to step aside and let them learn*, Jossey-Bass, San Francisco

Brookfield, S (1986) *Understanding and Facilitating Adult Learning: A comprehensive analysis of principles and effective practices*, Open University Press, Buckingham

Sims, N H (2006) *How to Run a Great Workshop: The complete guide to designing and running brilliant workshops and meetings*, Prentice Hall, Harlow

Lecturing –
tips and pitfalls

53

X-REF TOOL

49   Reference list of learning and development methods

The lecture has not enjoyed a good reputation in learning and develop-ment; it is often criticized for being too didactic, leaving learners too passive; and it is contrasted with facilitation, which is seen as the more learner-centred alternative. Yet the lecture is one of the longest-established methods of learning, and still has its place; a good lecturer can make a last-ing impression, and a stimulating lecture can be the catalyst for valuable learning. As with coaching and facilitation, much has been written about lecturing, and this book is not the place to attempt to distil the method, but a practical aid is to have a core list of some of the best tips to make use of and some of the worst pitfalls to avoid.

The top five tips are:

1   Speak clearly, slowly (but not too slowly) and loudly enough for those at the back to hear without deafening those at the front. Getting this right takes practice, and where possible rehearsal, and it's always worth taking feedback early in the lecture to make sure these basics are right. Make eye contact with the learners, and don't be over-dependent on notes.

2   Try to be learner centred. Just because lecturing is essentially a didactic activity doesn't mean it needs to be lecturer centred. Ask questions of the learners, perhaps to seek confirmation from their experiences, perhaps just to ensure the lecture is being understood, and always invite questions and comments at the end. As a general rule, always try to see the lecture from the learner's perspective.

3   Refresh, revise and renew. When a lecture is repeated, there is a danger it becomes stale and ceases to have relevance. The lecturer

should revisit the content and presentation of any lecture that is delivered repeatedly, and be prepared to make changes.

4 Use audio-visual aids wherever they can add value. This includes presentation slides, especially of pictorial or diagrammatic material, sound or video clips, objects or models, and even volunteers from the audience to demonstrate a point. This will add variety and will appeal to learners who favour a visual or auditory learning style.

5 Be honest, open and authentic. Where lecturers inject their own bias, they should be clear that is the case. Offer opinions, as long as they are distinguished from facts, but personalize wherever possible, as this can bring things to life.

The worst five pitfalls are:

1 Avoid 'death by PowerPoint'. Don't have too many slides, and don't use them as a prompt. Visual aids should support the lecture, not replace it or detract from it. Aim to keep down the amount of text on any slides that are used, and opt for pictorial imagery wherever possible.

2 Don't simply repeat what is available as reading material to support the lecture, even if the learners haven't seen the reading beforehand. The function of the lecture isn't to replace reading, but to complement it, and should focus on what the reading doesn't cover.

3 Avoid irritating habits like jangling keys or change in pockets, repeating the same clichés or catchphrases, verbal tics, or making extravagant gestures. These can be very distracting for learners. Perhaps a plant in the audience can point out things like this afterwards.

4 Never assume prior knowledge. If in doubt, test for it first by asking. Assuming knowledge where there is none, or it is imperfect, runs the risk of leaving the learners behind.

5 Avoid the surprise tactic. There will be occasional exceptions to this rule, but usually it is better to make points clearly and up front, like headlines at the start of a newspaper article, rather than burying the key message later in the lecture. The learner shouldn't have to work too hard to understand what the lecture is about. This reflects the old saw 'Tell 'em what you're going to tell 'em; tell 'em; then tell 'em what you've told them.'

FURTHER READING

Aarabi, P (2007) *The Art of Lecturing: A practical guide to successful university lectures and business presentations*, Cambridge University Press, Cambridge
Bligh, D (2000) *What's the Use of Lectures?*, Jossey-Bass, New York
Gaw, A (2010) *Our Speaker Today: A guide to effective lecturing*, SA Press, Glasgow
Race, P (2006) *The Lecturer's Toolkit*, Routledge, Abingdon
http://www.brookes.ac.uk/services/ocsd/2_learntch/20reasons.html (accessed December 2010)

How to mentor someone

54

X-REF TOOLS

22 The five aspects of talent management
23 The talent web
51 Coaching – tips and pitfalls

One of the oldest known ways of learning something is to follow the example of another. Craft apprenticeships from medieval times to the industrial era were founded on the principle of the novice being apprenticed to a journeyman, an experienced craftsman who passed on his knowledge and skill by example: the apprentice would observe and copy the journeyman, and be instructed and advised by him (it was usually a 'him'). Patronage, as a system, has an even older heritage: people in leading positions have often adopted protégés, or those whom they sought to help advance their careers. Patronage is sometimes viewed in a negative light, as nepotism, favouritism, or fostering undeserving advantage for unfair reasons, but when based on meritocratic criteria, and to address organizational needs, patronage has distinct benefits.

This is where mentoring comes in. One of the leading authorities on the subject, David Clutterbuck, argues that mentoring is the most cost-efficient and sustainable method of fostering and developing talent within an organization – quite a claim when one considers all the other available tools. Clutterbuck distinguishes mentoring from the related tools of coaching and counselling, as being focused not on specific tasks or functions, but on the development of the subject, through looking at the person's capability, potential and career-related personal development.

Mentoring is the process whereby the learner – or in this context the mentee – is supported and encouraged by a mentor to manage his or her own learning, in order to develop skills, achieve career goals and maximize potential. Organizations promote mentoring schemes because they want to harmonize this with their corporate objectives, and it fits very comfortably with a talent management approach. It's learner centred; it's intensive and one to one; it's flexible, encompassing a wide range of activities; and it's very powerful.

The mentor–mentee relationship works well because it is outside the line management relationship, although often still within the organization, at least if the organization is large, because it gives the more experienced mentor the chance to offer the mentee the benefit of his or her experience, and because it allows exactly the right scope for the mentee to choose options and directions, and gain confidence.

It can also be very empowering and developmental for the mentor, who may have had similar experiences to the mentee and may develop a strong sense of empathy.

The mentoring process involves a fairly simple series of meetings, discussions, goal setting and reviews. Mentors may need to draw upon their networks of contacts to give mentees access to developmental situations and experiences, but the real challenge for mentors is in harnessing the range of support skills they need.

Bob Aubrey and Paul Cohen identify five skills, which they describe as follows:

- *accompanying* – which is about making a commitment to, and going on a journey with, the mentee;
- *sowing* – which is about preparing the mentee for things he or she is not yet ready for, or doesn't yet understand;
- *catalysing* – which is about sparking action at a chosen moment, perhaps without having prepared the mentee;
- *showing* – which is about what the mentor does as much as says, offering the mentee an example; and
- *harvesting* – which is about helping the mentee to draw conclusions and inferences, learn from the experience and apply the learning to new situations.

There may be many more skills beyond these five, and the mentor should seek them out. This, then, is how to mentor someone: to take an active role and be prepared to make a number of differing interventions as appropriate to needs and circumstances.

FURTHER READING

Alred, G (2010) *The Mentoring Pocketbook*, Management Pocketbooks, Alresford

Aubrey, R and Cohen, P (1995) *Working Wisdom*, Jossey-Bass, San Francisco

Clutterbuck, D (1998) *Learning Alliances*, CIPD, London

Kay, D and Hinds, R (2009) *A Practical Guide to Mentoring: How to help others achieve their goals*, How To Books, Oxford

Whittaker, M and Cartwright, A (2000) *The Mentoring Manual*, Gower, Aldershot

http://www.coachingnetwork.org.uk/

How to organize work-based learning

55

X-REF TOOLS

33 Using different approaches to learning and development

56 Guided practice

69 Volunteering-based learning

A key problem with any sort of off-the-job learning – whether it's classroom based, online or something else, even if it's in a simulator – is transfer of learning from the artificial environment of the learning to the real environment of the job. Work-based learning is the solution to this problem: instead of undertaking learning in an alternative environment, work-based learning uses the real, live setting of work in the workplace to give learners the full experience and test their actual performance.

This would seem to imply that all learning for work should be work-based learning, but there are good reasons why this is not always applicable. It may not be safe to expose learners to the real work situation without some preparation; learners need to be protected. It may be too risky in terms of potential costs; learners could incur significant expense through their errors. It may simply be that learners need theory before they can practise; this is a matter of proper preparation. Or it may be that there are scenarios to explore that cannot be easily replicated in the workplace – pilots should practise emergency landings in a simulator, not in a real aeroplane at a real airfield.

Yet work-based learning, where feasible, can be very powerful. The following seven issues need to be considered:

1 Set aside time for the learning. There must be sufficient time for learners to absorb the learning and, crucially, to practise as much as they need.

2 Introduce the learning properly, so that the learners know what is involved and what is expected of them. Cover all the necessary

information about the workspace, equipment or machinery, materials or consumables, and the involvement of other people.

3 Explain first, then demonstrate, and repeat as necessary. It is important both to describe and show *what* has to be done and to explain *why*.

4 Let the learners try it. Wherever possible, try not to intervene too much: the learners need to take responsibility for their actions, to have a sense of control and build their self-confidence.

5 Repeat as necessary. Repeated instruction, demonstration and practice are all important.

6 Test understanding. Ask questions of the learners, ask them to undertake parts of the task out of sequence, and explore the limits of their knowledge and skill. This helps focus on areas for further development and improvement.

7 Review how well the lesson has worked and consider what more needs to be done or what needs to be done differently.

These seven issues may be seen as an adaptation of the learning and development cycle, applied specifically to the needs of work-based learning.

FURTHER READING

Milton, N (2010) *The Lessons Learned Handbook: Practical knowledge-based approach to learning from experience*, Chandos, Oxford

Rothwell, W and Kazanas, H (2004) *Improving On-the-Job Training: How to establish and operate a comprehensive OJT program*, Jossey-Bass, San Francisco

Sisson, G (2001) *Hands-On Training: A simple and effective method for on-the-job training*, Berrett-Koehler, San Francisco

Walter, D (2001) *Training on the Job*, ASTD Press, Alexandria, VA

Guided practice

56

Occupational learning and development is usually about learning how to do something, about becoming more proficient at demonstrating skills and fulfilling tasks. Practice has an important role to play in this, just as it does in learning to play a musical instrument, or perform dance or drama, or undertake sport or athletics.

But practice cannot simply be about constantly repeating the same actions or behaviours, as if these are practised incorrectly the final performance will be at best flawed. This is where guidance comes in: this is where the person responsible for the learning and development guides the learner, correcting mistakes as they arise and ensuring practice leads to competence and accomplishment. This has parallels with one-to-one support methods, such as coaching and mentoring, but the critical difference is that this tool is about supporting the learner in actual performance of the role or function.

Roberto Moretti has broken down what is involved in practice, to help both learners and whoever is guiding them. His starting point is the model of competence that describes how learners move from unconscious incompetence (they don't know what they don't know) to conscious incompetence (they know what they don't know) to conscious competence (they have to think about what they're doing) to unconscious competence (they perform tasks without consciously thinking about what they're doing).

Moretti's five processes for efficient practice are practical steps to follow to move through the competence model, and as such are invaluable for those managing work-based learning, or anyone who wants to learn a new skill. They're also a useful antidote to those who perceive learning as being simply about information transfer, as they explain what learning for work is really about – applying knowledge and developing your skills.

The five processes are:

- *identification* – where learners clarify what it is they are going to practise;
- *isolation* – where learners focus on an element small enough to practise to perfection;
- *reinforcement* – where learners repeatedly practise to get it right;
- *integration* – where learners link each practised element of skill to another, to accomplish more complex, or higher-level, skills;
- *escalation* – where learners build on the skill to begin to tackle new skills.

Moretti's classification of these processes is a valuable tool for helping make a success of guided practice.

FURTHER READING

Moretti, R (2009) *Practice Made Perfect*
http://www.practicebasedlearning.org

Putting together action learning sets

57

X-REF TOOLS

9 Kolb's experiential learning cycle

55 How to organize work-based learning

69 Volunteering-based learning

While action learning may be undertaken by individuals on their own, it is much more typically a group activity, where a group of colleagues, perhaps a work team or a community of professionals, come together in action learning sets. These sets exchange experiences of real work problems or challenges, ask questions of one another to review every aspect, consider solutions and try to implement them and move on to the next problem or challenge. These sets may be self-directed, or may be led and supported by a facilitator.

Sometimes action learning takes place off the job, in meeting rooms, but it can also be undertaken in the workplace, as Japanese companies in particular have shown. This makes sense, as its essence is about addressing real and specific work-based issues and situations.

The practical benefits are not confined to the solutions generated and applied to the problems and challenges examined; a further benefit is that the participants learn how to solve problems, and can apply these skills to future issues in their job or career.

Reginald Revans, in pioneering work for the Mining Association of Great Britain in 1945, is credited with first developing action learning, although it did not become popular or widespread until at least the 1960s, and most of Revans's academic work, and his founding of the Action Learning Trust, came later. It has been contrasted with traditional off-the-job learning, such as coursework, which it views as too theoretical and insufficiently rooted in practical reality. Revans's formula was that $L = P + Q$, where L stands for learning, and the other side of the equation is represented by programming, a rather outdated term referring to embedded knowledge, and questioning.

As the tool has developed through use, some have added R to Revans's formula, to represent reflection (see tool 9), and more generally the scope of inquiry of action learning sets has expanded.

Some practitioners emphasize the process of 'unlearning' as a first stage in action learning, where action learning set participants are encouraged to dispense with their preconceived ideas about a subject. This serves to 'clear the decks' and encourage fresh perspectives.

It is possible to pursue action learning in a more open way, and with few constraints on the way the work of the set develops. Some common ground rules, or ethics, for action learning include:

- confidentiality within the set;
- equality among set members;
- shared responsibility for the work of the set;
- consensus about outcomes and results.

Action learning sets may be formed for different reasons, which should influence which participants are selected. If the aim is to tackle a problem in a specific work area, then the work team located there may all gather in the set. Or it may be that an interdisciplinary team from across the organization needs to be put together to bring a range of skills to the set. A further possibility is that the set could be a means to encourage closer cooperation among work colleagues who have not been as collaborative as the organization needs them to be. Sometimes professionals with a shared interest, but from many different organizations, can form a set purely around a specific issue or small group of issues. The set may include employees from roughly the same level in an organization, or they can cut across hierarchies. This is not an exhaustive range of possibilities, but shows the sort of considerations that may influence the formation of a set.

On the basis that most learning and development are ultimately about action, rather than knowledge, action learning perhaps ought to be more commonly used than it is. Other than among its small circle of devotees, it remains an underutilized tool.

FURTHER READING

McGill, I and Brockbank, A (2003) *The Action Learning Handbook: Powerful techniques for education, professional development and training*, Routledge, Abingdon
Mumford, A (ed) (1997) *Action Learning at Work*, Gower, Aldershot
Pedler, M (2008) *Action Learning for Managers*, Gower, Aldershot
Revans, R (1980) *Action Learning: New techniques for management*, Blond & Briggs, London
http://www.cipd.co.uk/subjects/lrnanddev/general/actionlearning.htm (accessed November 2010)

Setting up a community of practice

58

X-REF TOOLS

14 How to develop a learning culture
15 How to develop a learning organization
75 Networking via professional bodies
78 Social networking and collaborative tools

Communities of practice, as Etienne Wenger explains, are groups of people with not just shared interests, but a shared stake in applying those interests to both practical and theoretical activity. They have a big emphasis on learning and on sharing the results of learning. Wenger propounds a social theory of learning: that it is not primarily an individual activity, but rather is something we do together.

Communities of practice (CoP) may be encouraged and developed among work colleagues within an organization, perhaps involving similar work teams from multiple locations, or among professionals of a particular discipline across many organizations, or among people from different organizations who share similar goals or values. For example, as a member of the Chartered Institute of Personnel and Development, I am part of a UK-wide community of practice involving thousands of HR and learning and development professionals.

Lately, CoPs have become confused with the technologies that support them. The digital revolution has enabled communities of practice, across organizational and national boundaries, to an unprecedented extent. But the likes of wikis, blogs and online discussion forums are simply tools to facilitate social learning and to help communities of practice, not the communities themselves. Technologists have found to their cost that CoPs cannot be created by putting in place software architecture; the communities have to want to exist and interact before they are given the tools to do so, not the other way around.

Establishing a CoP from scratch depends upon identifying a shared need, and in fact it is rare for them to be established in this contrived way – they are much more likely to grow organically.

However, if a prospective community is identified within a circle of like-minded people, there are a number of steps that may be taken to support their development. Wenger offers seven actions to cultivate CoPs, but these may be boiled down to just three. The first of these is to recognize and articulate the shared need, perhaps naming the community or crafting a mission statement for it. This will be more powerful if it is initiated or carried out by the community itself. The second step is to give the community resources, and not necessarily in the form of software. Time is the most valuable resource: the time for people to spend bringing the group together. Other useful resources could be staff, premises or a financial budget. The third step is to give moral support, and this is most valuable when it comes from senior managers or other decision makers; the community will thrive if it feels valued.

Interventions to offer these steps may be made even with organically developing CoPs, and at any stage of their development. The benefits will be repaid in the ideas, initiatives and innovations generated by the CoP. A key concept for this is the creation of social capital – the outputs of the shared learning and the value both individuals and the collective derive from being part of a CoP.

FURTHER READING

Wenger, E (1999) *Communities of Practice: Learning, meaning, and identity*, Cambridge University Press, Cambridge

Wenger, E, White, N and Smith, J (2009) *Digital Habitats: Stewarding technology for communities*, CPsquare, Portland, OR

http://www.ewenger.com/

The seven pillars of a corporate university

59

X-REF TOOLS

14 How to develop a learning culture
15 How to develop a learning organization
87 How to get value from a corporate university

There are seven critical success factors involved in the establishment of any corporate university that aims to develop learning and knowledge for the organization, its constituent employees and perhaps a broader community (suppliers, partners, customers, shareholders, employees' families, etc) – and to do so with the same levels of professionalism found in a respected academic university. I call these the seven pillars of the corporate university (with apologies to T E Lawrence). The seven are:

1 strategy setting;
2 project planning;
3 branding;
4 infrastructure;
5 curriculum;
6 learning programmes and support;
7 assessment and accreditation.

1 *Strategy setting*. Why a corporate university? What is it for? What will it do? What are its aims, and how should they be expressed? The answers to these questions should lead to the formulation of a strategy.

2 *Project planning*. This should take account of the available personnel and resources and how they are to be deployed. It should follow a

series of carefully determined milestones that mark the way along the set-up timetable. There should be an evaluation of the risk attached to any of the milestones slipping, and contingency plans for how to get back on track if anything should go awry.

3 *Branding.* There is an opportunity here to build on the corporate brand and its values, and to position learning in such a way that it is understood as part of the strategic purpose of the organization. An important part of the concept of creating a corporate university is its symbolism, and the inspirational effect it has on its learners and contributors – the brand is critical to this.

4 *Infrastructure.* This should be simple and intuitive, but serve the potential needs of the entire learner population. It should include a budget, a resourcing plan and all the management planning of any comparable initiative (including learner support systems, both for traditional, face-to-face learning and for online learning), and all the associated documentation, such as an application process.

5 *Curriculum.* The curriculum defines the scope of what the university will teach (and research); it also defines a range of courses (and other learning initiatives), their learner objectives, and how they will be provided. A classification of the subject range that will be offered can help clarify people's understanding of the scope of the university, even if the detailed content is not yet in place.

6 *Learning programmes and support.* A corporate university needs to specify not just the content on offer, but the form it will take. As a minimum, it should include: facilities for face-to-face courses, which give it a physical presence; a digital presence, including online courses and online learning resources; links to other learning approaches, especially coaching and work-based learning; and potential for more, such as innovative approaches to learning. Thought also needs to be given to the range of different kinds of support, including tutoring and mentoring, and the roles of line managers.

7 *Assessment and accreditation.* Assessment and accreditation partnerships underscore a corporate university's sustainability, provide clear success measures and help motivate learners. There should be links with professional bodies and their continuous professional development programmes, and links with an academic institution to confer degrees and other awards.

FURTHER READING

The description of this tool is based on an article that originally appeared at http://www.learnforever.co.uk/articles/The_Seven_Pillars_of_the_Corporate_University.pdf (accessed December 2010).

Allen, M (ed) (2007) *The Next Generation of Corporate Universities: Innovative approaches for developing people and expanding organizational capabilities*, Pfeiffer, San Francisco

Paton, R *et al* (eds), *Handbook of Corporate University Development: Managing strategic learning initiatives in public and private domains*, Gower, Aldershot

Walton, J (1999) Human resource development and the corporate university, Ch 16 in *Strategic Human Resource Development*, FT Prentice Hall, Harlow

Wheeler, K and Clegg, E (2005) *The Corporate University Workbook: Launching the 21st century learning organization*, Jossey-Bass, San Francisco

60 Preparing a lesson plan

X-REF TOOLS

31 A step-by-step guide to planning a learning event

61 Preparing to deliver a course: a checklist

81 Assessing learning

On first sight, this tool looks as though it belongs in the planning part of this book. Arguably, all aspects of planning and preparing, developing and designing learning belong to the second phase of the learning and development cycle. But the lesson plan is the tool that guides both the trainer and the learner through implementation of the learning, and as such it makes sense to include it here.

Preparation of a lesson plan begins by setting aims and objectives. These are a response to learner needs and provide a clear direction for everything else in the plan. In this sense, the lesson plan is an articulation of the learning and development cycle, specifying the aims, stating how they will be met and providing a framework for evaluation. The lesson plan should state the overall aim(s) of the lesson, and detail the more specific learner objectives.

From the objectives, the next step is to describe the way the lesson will meet them, including describing the content and activities. This lies at the heart of the lesson plan, and could be said to be its most important aspect, as long as it is placed in its proper context. It involves considering the best way for the participants to learn the things they need to learn, including ensuring that the blend of inputs and activities is sufficiently varied to maintain everyone's interest. Some lesson plans divide this part into *what* will be learnt (the content) and *how* it will be learnt (the activities or process).

Closely linked to this is a clear indication of timings. The lesson plan should estimate how long each part of the plan should take, creating a timetable for the learning event. This should include setting aside enough time for the appropriate breaks for meals or refreshments, or even just short comfort breaks to allow for a little relaxation.

The lesson plan should also include a clear statement of responsibilities, clearly indicating who will undertake each part. Where the event is simply a short face-to-face training session facilitated by one trainer, this may seem self-explanatory, especially if it is the same trainer who is writing the lesson plan. However, the lesson plan should be a document that may be shared among a team of trainers or passed on from one to another.

Resources should also be identified for each part of the lesson plan. These should include: the premises, furnishings and ancillary facilities; any essential equipment, such as a computer and projector or a flipchart easel; any books or workbooks; and all consumable materials of any kind. Everything that is essential for the success of the lesson should be specified in the plan.

Lastly, the lesson plan should make clear how the learning will be assessed and evaluated, linking back to the objectives.

The format of the lesson plan doesn't matter. My preference is to lay out the information in a table, one column for objectives, one for content and activities, one for resources, etc, but any format that clearly shows the relationship between each of the elements is fine.

FURTHER READING

Most of the available resources on this topic are aimed at teachers in a classroom setting, but trainers should be able to translate the ideas to their contexts.

Haynes, A (2007) *100 Ideas for Lesson Planning*, Continuum International Publishing, London

Karper, N (2010) *Lesson Plans Writing: How to write a good lesson plan and avoid common mistakes*, Psylon Press

Ryan, M and Serdyukov, P (2007) *Writing Effective Lesson Plans: The 5-star approach*, Allyn & Bacon, Boston, MA

61 Preparing to deliver a course: a checklist

The success of a course depends more than anything else upon planning and preparation on the part of the trainer, lecturer or facilitator of the course. The things to be considered when preparing to deliver a course, or any kind of face-to-face, off-the-job learning intervention, may be classified into four groups: the people, the information, the facilities, and the methods and media:

The people:

- Consider everyone who needs to attend the course, including the facilitator(s), learners and any others (such as guest speakers, management representatives, etc).

- If anyone else is likely to attend, even for part of the course, consideration needs to be given to how they may be accommodated.

- Everyone's role needs to be made clear.

- The facilitator needs to have all the relevant background information about all of the participants.

- Advance thought needs to be given to whether any of the participants have any special needs.
- Everyone needs to be welcomed on arrival.

The information:

- Joining instructions must be issued to learners in advance, including a timetable to enable them to plan their attendance, how to get there, what to expect and how to prepare.
- The venue and any refreshments, meals, accommodation or parking must be booked. The facilitator should hold copies of all relevant booking information.
- If there is any pre-course work, everyone must receive it in good time.
- Everyone else who needs to know about the course (eg participants' managers) should receive sufficient advance information.

The facilities:

- There must be a principal course room.
- There may need to be a number of nearby syndicate rooms to break out into.
- There ought to be a separate place for refreshment breaks, and access to fresh air.
- There ought to be a restaurant or other facility for meals.
- There may need to be overnight accommodation.
- There should be handy car parking and/or clear access by public transport.
- There must be conveniently located toilets, including disabled facilities.
- There must be clear directions about emergency procedures.
- Special consideration must be given to whether all of the facilities are accessible for those with mobility issues. There may be a need to provide additional facilities for other special needs, such as induction loops for those with hearing difficulties.

The methods and media:

- There must be appropriate equipment, such as a computer, multimedia projector or SMART Board, screen(s), flipchart easel and paper, etc. This equipment will need to be checked to ensure it is in working order.
- There must be an adequate supply of handouts or other materials for learners.
- There may need to be books, manuals, DVDs, etc.

- If access is required to the web or other networks, an internet connection will be needed, and will need to be checked in advance to make sure it works properly.
- Other required materials may include a pointer, flipchart pens, fixatives such as Blu-Tack, extra paper, spare pens and pencils, or other stationery.

Finally, consider whether there is anything else that may have been forgotten.

FURTHER READING

Daines, J, with Daines, C and Graham, B (2006) *Adult Learning, Adult Teaching*, Welsh Academic Press, Cardiff

Gravells, A (2008) *Preparing to Teach in the Lifelong Learning Sector*, Learning Matters, Exeter

http://honolulu.hawaii.edu/intranet/committees/FacDevCom/guidebk/ teachtip/teachtip.htm (accessed December 2010)

Tips for team teaching

62

X-REF TOOLS

52 Facilitation – tips and pitfalls
53 Lecturing – tips and pitfalls

When more than one teacher, trainer or instructor cooperates to deliver or facilitate a learning event, the process is usually described as team teaching. Where resources are scarce, this may seem wasteful, but there are many situations where it is essential, and still more where it is very helpful to have two or more people sharing the teaching or training roles.

This tool comprises some handy tips and advice for making team teaching work well:

- *Plan thoroughly*. It won't work if the facilitation team just turns up. A sole trainer who knows his or her subject well may sometimes be able to get away with limited preparation and improvising on the day, but this won't work with two separate minds involved, even (especially?) if both are experts in the field. The facilitation team need to get together before the learning event and talk about who does what and how the two will complement each other, identify any potential differences or areas of conflict and agree how these will be handled.

- *One leads, one sweeps*. The simplest formula for each session is for one facilitator to take the lead role and the other to 'take a back seat'. The leader's role is clear; the sweeper's is more complicated: looking for missed points, things that have been glossed over too quickly, or anything where the learners don't all seem to fully understand. The sweeper should be prepared to interject to clarify things, and the leader should be prepared to accept these interjections.

- *Back each other up.* It doesn't do to have unrehearsed differences at the learning event, and the facilitation team should always be prepared to back each other up. This instils confidence, and builds a sense of cohesion and teamwork that spreads from the facilitation team to the learners themselves.

- *Cooperate, don't compete.* The facilitation team should work together, and shouldn't compete for the learners' attention or set themselves up against each other, except in the instance below.

- *Compare and contrast.* Often there isn't a right or wrong answer to a problem. In this sort of situation it pays to take differing or opposing views and promote a debate. A polemic between two facilitators can stimulate the learners and inject a lively atmosphere into a session. The facilitation team should plan where and when they are going to use this tactic, but a team experienced in working together may be able to do so spontaneously, if they spot an opportunity.

- *Offer variety.* Use differing styles to offer learners variety. Where one of the facilitation team is more didactic and another more facilitative, this sort of difference may play to different learning styles and work to the advantage of the learning outcomes. Even the simple act of switching which facilitator leads each session can enliven an otherwise dull session.

- *Support specific learners.* One tactic that sometimes works is for the facilitators to agree in advance that one of them will offer more support to certain learners in the group, while the other supports the rest. This needn't be a secretive process, and it may be agreed in advance, or on the day, with the learners. Some learners enjoy the sense of having a dedicated support person available.

There will be many other techniques and tactics a facilitation team may deploy. These are just some examples.

FURTHER READING

Buckley, F (1999) *Team Teaching: What, why, and how?*, Sage Publications, Thousand Oaks, CA

360-degree feedback

63

X-REF TOOLS

   3 L&DNA grids
  13 Johari window

The 360 degrees of the name of this tool describe a circle, a complete circle, from which feedback may be drawn. The idea is to elicit feedback from everyone around the subject in an organization: the subject's line manager, subordinates, immediate colleagues and team members, internal and perhaps external customers or suppliers, and anyone else who has direct contact with the subject.

The origins of the term are sometimes explained like this: 90 degrees describe the narrow section of a circle formed when one colleague gives feedback to another; 180 degrees describe the reciprocal process when the two colleagues give feedback to each other, but this is still only half of the picture; 270 degrees add to the circle in drawing feedback from others; and 360 degrees complete the circle to present the full picture. Another name for this tool is multi-rater feedback.

The most common context for 360-degree feedback is performance development and review. Instead of a subjective, perhaps biased, assessment by a line manager, 360 degrees is believed to give a more rounded view. However, the accumulation of several subjective perspectives does not necessarily add up to an objective assessment, but merely eliminates the most obvious expression of bias. Like repertory grids, it provides more information, which must be interpreted carefully.

Another problem is that it can be a very time-consuming process, and prior to the development of web-based systems it generated a disproportionate volume of paperwork. It is also expensive, as a lot of staff time is taken up, before any consideration of the costs of software systems or the support of external consultants.

Like anything associated with appraisal of performance, it needs to be implemented sensitively, to avoid hostile reactions and destructive behaviour, but if this hurdle is overcome it can be very motivating and empowering for participants, especially where it is implemented consistently for everyone in the organization. It is in widespread use by many of the leading companies in the world.

As a learning and development tool, 360-degree feedback needs to move beyond simply informing performance appraisal and have a clearly developmental focus. Where this is the case, advocates are very enthusiastic about the impact of this tool: in the research I conducted for this book, when people were canvassed for their favourite tools this was the one that received the most acclaim. The big issue seems to be that, where development recommendations arising from the feedback are acted upon, participants can see that their contributions are taken seriously and can have a strong sense that they, and their opinions, are valued.

FURTHER READING

Bracken, D *et al* (1997) *Should 360-Degree Feedback Be Used Only for Developmental Purposes?*, Center for Creative Leadership, Greensboro, NC

Lepsinger, R and Lucia, A (2009) *The Art and Science of 360 Degree Feedback*, Jossey-Bass, San Francisco

Peacock, T (2007) *The 360 Degree Feedback Pocketbook*, Management Pocketbooks, Alresford

http://humanresources.about.com/od/360feedback/a/360feedback.htm (accessed November 2010)

http://www.cipd.co.uk/subjects/perfmangmt/appfdbck/360fdbk.htm (accessed November 2010)

Psychometric instruments for development rather than assessment

64

Psychometric instruments are used extensively in people management, but usually for recruitment or selection, as they are primarily assessment tools. However, there is plenty of scope to use them developmentally.

Early psychometrics, with their focus on outdated notions of intelligence, are largely discredited, but modern tools are rigorously tested for reliability and validity (see, for example, the USA's Standards for Educational and Psychological Testing) and have a clearer purpose and function. Psychometric instruments can objectively measure an individual's preferences, predominant personality traits, aptitudes for certain tasks or roles, and capabilities in certain skills. Among the most popular tools are 16PF, where PF stands for personality factors, the Occupational Personality Questionnaire, or OPQ, and the Myers–Briggs Type Indicator, or MBTI.

Psychometric instruments can support development in several ways:

- Just as universities frequently use them to support career planning and development for new graduates or soon-to-be graduates, so employers can use them to support career and succession planning within the organization. The tests can help learners make more informed choices about their options, based on a match of their characteristics and preferences with the features of job roles. Thus psychometric instruments contribute to talent management.

- Coaching has a natural affinity with psychometric instruments, as coaches may administer and score tests, and learners can discuss with them their experience of the tests and what they think about the outcomes. Passmore (2008) cites several examples of the use of instruments in coaching, including the OPQ and the MBTI. The instruments can provide some objective data, which can help depersonalize some discussions and provide a series of topics to structure the discussions.

- Development centres draw heavily upon psychometric instruments, among a battery of different resources, to encourage intensive self-examination and group work (see tool 70 for more details).

- Psychometric instruments can even contribute to coursework, used sparingly and as a complement to other activities.

Illustrative example

An oil drilling technologies company uses the Myers–Briggs Type Indicator for management development. A coach from the learning department meets individually with all the managers to clarify their goals for development within the company, and the managers self-assess their personality type. Then they take the test for a more objective reporting of their type. Shortly afterwards, they meet again with the coach to debrief and consider how these findings relate to the managers' work. The managers are then left to apply these ideas and think about how they affect their managerial behaviour.

Organizations that find these tools particularly useful can explore other ways of including them in their employee development activities.

FURTHER READING

Passmore, J (ed) (2008) *Psychometrics in Coaching: Using psychological and psychometric tools for development*, Kogan Page, London
http://www.apa.org/science/programs/testing/standards.aspx (accessed December 2010)

65 Innovative approaches to learning

X-REF TOOLS

2 Understanding learning, development, education and training

8 Informal and non-formal learning

19 Gardner's multiple intelligences

33 Using different approaches to learning and development

Most people who work in learning and development will have reflected, at one time or another, on their schooldays and on their learning experiences at school. Many will also have given thought to what school meant to their employees or trainees. As the first formal, organized learning that most of us experience, school leaves its imprint on our attitudes to learning and on our expectations of education and training.

Unfortunately, for many people, school is not a positive experience. Many young people choose to leave school as soon as they are legally able, and some absent themselves even earlier. Some of those who stay on, even into further and higher education, do so reluctantly, regarding education as a necessary evil. We know that many people come to adult learning situations carrying this legacy of suspicion and resentment, and the first battle we face is trying to get these people to engage with the learning process.

Yet the first experiences people have of in-company training often reinforce their prejudices. They are herded into classrooms or hotel rooms, sit facing a flipchart, whiteboard or projection screen, follow a timetable, and are 'taught'. The curriculum may be different – instead of maths, English and geography, there is team building, customer focus and communication – but the approach is essentially the same. This kind of corporate training is, in fact, not very different from the school experience that people perceive has failed them.

Yet course facilitators can choose to use anything to facilitate a course, and courses are far from the only means we can offer people to learn. Variety is much more than just a means of keeping learners awake; creativity in learning techniques sparks creativity in the workplace. Sometimes the innovative use of techniques will inspire employees to innovate at work, while occasionally they will be able to directly use techniques that they have experienced through the learning opportunity, such as brainstorming or mind mapping. Often the best way to get people to work effectively and to make a greater contribution to an organization is to tap into their creativity – using both the left and right sides of the brain (see tool 8) – to unlock and develop their potential. Among the many possibilities are:

- drama, or amateur theatre, including dramatic representations of topical events in the workplace, perhaps led by professional actors, but always involving employees as active participants;
- the use of arts and crafts, to demonstrate the benefits of communication and coaching, to encourage creativity, individual goal setting and attainment, and to show the impact of teamwork;
- the outdoor environment, to provide a challenging (and healthy) context in which to foster cooperation, leadership and team building;
- sports and games, to encourage striving for goals, along with cooperation and teamwork, problem solving, leadership and imagination;
- music and dance, food and drink, magic, animal husbandry, or anything at all that inspires learners.

The more unusual the techniques are, the better, but the connecting thread is to find a means, or a context, that inspires learners, and exploit it. Once learners are engaged, that is half the battle, and people are much more likely to be engaged by things that interest and excite them than by yet another session sitting around a room with a flipchart or a PowerPoint projection.

Illustrative example

The Wizards Network is a group of consultants and specialists from other fields working together in the UK to bring innovation to their clients. One of their most popular offerings is the chocolate factory, an interactive learning experience involving small-scale manufacture of high-quality handmade chocolates. Participants design, manufacture and package their own sweets, using the finest fresh ingredients and the support of a professional chocolatier, in addition to a learning facilitator. The process enables learning in teamwork, communication, customer focus and other important disciplines, and often achieves high-impact business results, especially when tailored to address specific learning needs and objectives for the client company. The main reason it works is because learners are much more engaged than in a traditional learning experience, they are energized and, most of all, they have fun.

Among the objections to innovative approaches are that such activities are frivolous. In times of budgetary restraint, care must be taken not to spend more on the innovative solution than on the more traditional approach. The innovative approach should be subject to the same sort of evaluation, including financial evaluation, as all other approaches, and perhaps it pays to begin with mild innovation; once a successful precedent is established, more adventurous approaches can be adopted.

Another objection is that some options may seem resource-intensive, and indeed some are. Some may be more expensive than others. But if a cost–benefit analysis can prove their worth, this should not be an issue. If it is, then there are plenty of low-cost, low-resource options: using poetry and literature isn't likely to break the bank!

Perhaps it sounds like a lot of trouble? Executing a new and complicated delivery method may indeed be time-consuming, as is delivering classroom-based coursework for the first time, but practice makes each new challenge more straightforward than the last, and the experience is beneficial for the trainer. If something is particularly specialized, then the answer may be to find a specialist to do the job.

Innovative approaches to learning challenge us all. We are constantly learning new things about learning and development, the theory and practice are rapidly evolving, and this is especially true for learning methods. If we aren't moving forward and welcoming change, then we're standing still and getting left behind. To paraphrase Mary Lou Cook, learning is all about growing, inventing, taking risks and understanding the place of creativity in our whole lives – not just at home, at work or at school, but everywhere. Learning and development professionals need to take advantage of all the tools at their disposal.

FURTHER READING

Many of the ideas for this tool originally appeared in the following article in 2006: http://www.learnforever.co.uk/articles/Innovative_Approaches_to_Learning.pdf (accessed November 2010)

Using storytelling in learning and development

66

X-REF TOOL

65 Innovative approaches to learning

The ancient tale of Scheherazade is one of the most enduring of all stories, and one that explains the power of storytelling. In the tale, the shah of Persia takes a new wife every night and has her executed the next day, but Scheherazade manages to prolong her marriage by every night telling the shah a story so entrancing that he feels he has to keep her alive night after night, until, after one thousand and one nights, the shah spares Scheherazade's life and decides she must remain his queen.

Scheherazade had no modern audio-visual aids, but sustained her listener's interest, and fulfilled her aims, purely by the power of her storytelling to engage. On the other hand, we have all heard stories so dull they failed to capture our imagination or even our attention. The lesson is that storytelling needs to be compelling, and that if it is it can help accomplish great things.

Storytelling is an important part of our culture; we tend to associate it with childhood, but it remains very much a part of adult life as well. We repeat anecdotes about events that have meaning for us, we 'tell tales' and we construct stories to explain concepts. At work, stories reinforce and bring to life information otherwise conveyed in a dry, facts-and-figures format.

For learning, we can develop and embed knowledge better by offering it in the form of a story. All that is required for this is that those responsible for learning need to learn how to craft a story and how to tell it for maximum effect – and these skills can be acquired. The storyteller needs to do the following:

- Establish the theme or message of the story (this could be an important business message).
- Set the scene, describing the context and events leading up to the story (this could include the business background, such as a problem to be solved).
- Introduce the characters who populate the story, such as a hero and a villain.
- Narrate the sequence of events, including dilemmas and decisions, problems and solutions.
- Conclude the story and underline the message.

There are a limited number of story types; various theories reduce the basic number of storylines of all kinds to just seven. Margaret Parkin (2010) identifies storytelling applications for five categories in people development: dealing with change; being creative at work; developing leaders and team building; dealing with stress; and developing emotional intelligence.

We need a context in which to place storytelling, and this should include identifying meaningful stories for learning and development, introducing and telling those stories, inviting feedback, and redefining the stories in the light of others' experiences and applications. This gives us a useful perspective for introducing storytelling into our organizations.

FURTHER READING

Denning, S (2011) *The Leader's Guide to Storytelling: Mastering the art and discipline of business narrative*, Jossey-Bass, San Francisco

Gabriel, Y (2000) *Storytelling in Organizations: Facts, fictions, and fantasies*, Oxford University Press, Oxford

McDrury, J and Alterio, M (2003) *Learning through Storytelling in Higher Education: Using reflection and experience to improve learning*, Routledge, Abingdon

Parkin, M (2010) *Tales for Change: Using storytelling to develop people and organizations*, Kogan Page, London

Games, and learning through play

67

X-REF TOOLS

50 Icebreakers

65 Innovative approaches to learning

68 Simulation

Play, as any early years specialist will confirm, is crucial to how infants and children learn. It may not be essential for adults, but nonetheless it can be an invaluable tool in engaging adults with the learning process and perhaps evoking memories of early learning experiences. One of the main ways we play is through organized games, in their various forms, and game playing has a surprisingly long and honourable tradition in adult learning.

There are, broadly, four forms of games in widespread use:

- sports and outdoor games;
- board games and other resource-based games;
- role-playing games;
- computer-based and web-based games.

Sports and outdoor games are popular for the reason cited in tool 65, because they are popular activities for participants and thus engage them and put them in a good frame of mind for learning to take place. Sports and outdoor games also have a natural affinity with certain subjects, being excellent vehicles to explore leadership, team working, communication, goal setting, planning and execution of plans. A whole industry has grown up around organizations like Outward Bound that use the outdoor environment and activities like orienteering, climbing and canoeing to help develop self-awareness, team building and a set of management skills around overcoming challenges. This range of activities lends itself very readily to transfer to the sort of challenges that need to be overcome in the workplace.

Board games around enterprise development themes, taking their cue from the likes of Monopoly, used to be very popular, but have declined since computer-based games emerged with a far greater range and scope to simulate real work activities. Simpler versions remain common within coursework, where teams of learners often cooperate, and compete with other teams, in tasks like building a model bridge or designing a device to launch an egg. Events featuring this sort of activity are useful in forming and developing work teams. Other resource-based games include card games and variations of children's party games, using the materials that come to hand, such as furniture and stationery, to reduce work activities to simpler processes as models for learning.

Role playing is a kind of game playing, although many participants in this sort of activity, in courses run every day, may not recognize it as such. Role playing, where learners act out various scenarios, works well within courses and perhaps development centres as a means to explore interpersonal skills, including customer service and communication with colleagues.

In the last decade or so, computer-based games have brought game playing for learning back to the fore. Observers of software development have noted the phenomenal success of electronic games in engaging players and encouraging them to stay involved, to achieve the next goal or get to the next level. This engagement is what they have tried to transfer to digital games for learning. This has not been as successful as some had hoped, because in games for entertainment the point is just to get to the next level, whereas in games for learning there are learner objectives to achieve and prove. Nevertheless, computer-based games remain an invaluable learning tool, especially for a new generation of electronic games players, and an important part of the e-learning arsenal.

Altogether, games and play have the potential to enrich the learning experience and to make training activities more enjoyable and more effective.

FURTHER READING

El-Shamy, S (2001) *Training Games: Everything you need to know about using games to reinforce learning*, Stylus Publishing, Sterling, VA

El-Shamy, S (2005) *Role Play Made Easy: 25 structured rehearsals for managing problem situations and dealing with difficult people*, Jossey-Bass, San Francisco

El-Shamy, S and Stuebe, G (2000) *Card Games for Developing Teams*, Gower, Aldershot

Gibson, D, Aldrich, C and Prensky, M (2007) *Games and Simulations in Online Learning*, Information Science Publishing, Hershey, PA

Henriksen, T D (2010) *A Little More Conversation, a Little Less Action, Please: Rethinking learning games for organisational development and adult education*, Lambert Academic Publishing, Saarbrücken

Kroehnert, G (2002) *103 Additional Training Games*, McGraw-Hill, Roseville, NSW

Prensky, M (2001) *Digital Game-Based Learning*, McGraw-Hill, New York

http://www.thiagi.com/games.html (accessed December 2010)

68 Simulation

X-REF TOOLS

65 Innovative approaches to learning
67 Games, and learning through play

Simulation is a tool with a long history in learning and development. Ancient armies staged mock battles to simulate the conditions of real warfare. Medieval craftsmen built models to simulate what their real crafts would look like and to show how they would be constructed. And, in the popular imagination as well as in fact, flight simulators have been a common method for training aircraft pilots almost as long as aviation has existed.

The advent of the microprocessor has made computer-based simulations much more accessible, and has opened up a whole new era of simulation for learning purposes. Computer-based simulations, sometimes shortened to sims, can be as simple as animated graphs or diagrams that change as you adjust the spreadsheet variables, or more complex representations of real-life activities such as the operation of machinery or even virtual surgery or, as a further abstraction, representations of activities in an imaginary world.

The great benefit of simulation is that it can closely replicate the real work experience in a situation where the learner and others are protected from some of the pitfalls of real work, such as health and safety dangers and concerns, or the risk of incurring excessive costs or waste.

The International Virtual Medical School (IVIMEDS) was founded in Dundee in 2002, as a collaboration of university medical schools and institutions from around the world, committed to achieving maximum benefit from new educational technologies. One of IVIMEDS' earliest and most exciting initiatives was the development of virtual surgery online. This sought to simulate the conditions of a surgical theatre, where operations could be simulated on virtual patients, offering trainee surgeons the opportunity to practise their skills without threatening the lives of patients. The only previous alternative to this was practice on corpses, but these don't react in the same way as live people, whereas the simulations could be programmed to do so. Development of this facility has proved problematic, but remains an application of simulation to learning that has huge potential.

Simulation is a powerful tool for replicating real work and making learning for it more realistic, and significantly eases the problem of learning transfer, as the artificial situation so closely resembles the real one.

FURTHER READING

Aldrich, C (2005) *Learning by Doing: A comprehensive guide to simulations, computer games, and pedagogy in e-learning and other educational experiences*, Pfeiffer, San Francisco

Gibson, D, Aldrich, C and Prensky, M (2007) *Games and Simulations in Online Learning*, Information Science Publishing, Hershey, PA

http://www.atghome.com/simulation_white_paper.pdf (accessed December 2010)

http://www.ivimeds.org/

69 Volunteering-based learning

X-REF TOOLS

8 Informal and non-formal learning

55 How to organize work-based learning

When people undertake volunteering (also known as voluntary work), giving their time and effort without remuneration, they often apply their existing skills or acquire new skills, or both. Volunteering can be a great way to learn, and volunteering-based learning is for volunteers what work-based learning is for employees; in other words, knowledge and skills may be acquired from volunteering just as they may be acquired from work experience. Volunteering is a context for informal and non-formal learning.

Many people know from their own experience that there is a two-way flow between paid work and voluntary work. On the one hand, there are those who offer their career expertise to charities and to community initiatives *pro bono*, and on the other hand there are those, like interns, who undertake voluntary work in order to gain experience they need to pursue a paid career in a similar field. Sometimes these are even the same people.

The lesson for learning and development managers is that volunteering is an under-exploited means for employee development. It is not just about fulfilling corporate social responsibilities, but can be a means of developing employees' knowledge, skills and attitudes, as well as a source for acquiring skilled recruits.

In 2009, Volunteer Development Scotland created the brand name 'VSkills' to describe volunteering-based learning, and undertook a commission on behalf of the Scottish Government to develop an application of the concept to employability. The rationale was that the broad skills of employability, such as communication, working with others and problem solving, could be acquired from almost any volunteering experience. VSkills for Employability has enabled many volunteers to obtain credit, in the form of a nationally recognized qualification, for the skills they were already practising and demonstrating in their volunteering. These credits have been obtained without undertaking any further course or formal training – the volunteers have simply been assessed and accredited for the voluntary work they were doing anyway. At time of writing, Volunteer Development Scotland was planning to extend the VSkills concept into more specific occupational disciplines, such as retail qualifications for charity shop volunteers.

If an organization has not utilized volunteering-based learning before, it can be difficult to get started. There may be some blind alleys in identifying the right charitable, voluntary or community initiatives to develop partnerships with. In the UK and some other countries, local volunteer centres or bureaux can help make these links. With perseverance, organizations can find partners that can offer valuable development opportunities for their employees. Once this is established, its big advantage is that it is low-cost – there's an investment of time and effort, but rarely much direct expenditure in using volunteering-based learning.

FURTHER READING

Lynch, R and McCurley, S (2000) *Essential Volunteer Management*, Directory of Social Change, London

Stallings, B and Ellis, S (2010) *Leading the Way to Successful Volunteer Involvement: Practical tools for busy executives*, Energize, Philadelphia

70 Development centres

X-REF TOOLS

4 Identifying organizational learning needs: a step-by-step approach

22 The five aspects of talent management

24 The succession planning cycle

25 Devising and using standards of competence

64 Psychometric instruments for development rather than assessment

Development centres are concentrated multi-activity events, usually held within a single organization, taking place typically over two or three days, sometimes longer. Less common than assessment centres, they are a similar tool for a different purpose: assessment centres are used for recruitment and selection, whereas in development centres the participants are actively involved in the assessment of themselves and others as part of their personal and professional development. A key idea is to de-emphasize the assessment aspect and to help the participants relax; the event should feel more like a course and less like a selection interview.

Among the notable differences between assessment centres (ACs) and development centres (DCs) are: ACs have pass/fail criteria, and DCs do not; ACs are focused on selection, and DCs are focused on development; ACs tend to involve external candidates, and DCs usually involve internal candidates; ACs have a short-term focus, and DCs are more long-term oriented; ACs are more interested in current performance, and DCs are more interested in future potential; ACs sometimes give no feedback, and DCs always do.

Development centres may be deployed to support talent management and development, succession planning, and initiatives, or simply as a means of gathering information for learning and development needs analyses. They represent a tool for gaining a deeper understanding of the aspirations and abilities of a relatively small group, testing and stretching them, planning how their development may contribute to the organization, and in the process conveying a strong sense of value to the participants.

A development centre may include any of the following: briefings, group work, interviews, counselling, discussions, brainstorming, 360-degree feedback, exercises, activities, simulations, competence-based analyses and assessments, personal development planning, domain mapping (which involves targeting desired levels of knowledge and skills to be acquired) and the use of psychometric instruments. It may be supported before and after by the use of online resources, in the form of pre-centre readings, surveys, tests and activities for the participants.

It can be an expensive tool to deploy, because of the intensive scrutiny involved, which means there needs to be a large team of facilitators and observers, often as many as a one-to-one ratio to the participants. This means it needs to be carefully planned, to ensure a return of value commensurate with this significant investment. Perhaps the greatest advantage is that this is recognized by the participants, and so it can be very motivating to be selected to take part in a development centre, as this demonstrates that the organization thinks highly of participants and is planning a future for them.

FURTHER READING

Ballantyne, I and Povah, N (2004) *Assessment and Development Centres*, Gower, Aldershot

Woodruffe, C (2007) *Development and Assessment Centres: Identifying and developing competence*, Human Assets, London

71 Assessing and recording competence

48

X-REF TOOLS

25 Devising and using standards of competence

81 Assessing learning

Assessing and recording competence are both a means of recognizing the work standards employees have attained and a means of supporting their ongoing development. The first of these is not in itself particularly developmental, but is an essential prerequisite of planning future development; it establishes a baseline, and often the process of undergoing assessment can be developmental in its own right. The second of these addresses the more developmental purpose of assessing and recording competence, as it is the cornerstone of competence-based development for individuals and for organizations.

Assessment of competence may be conducted in various ways, but essentially comes down to two categories: the assessor looks at what the learner does, or conducts an observation of performance to prove competence; and the assessor considers a range of diverse evidence, by studying a learner portfolio. These two processes used to be enshrined, in the UK, in different qualification units for assessors. The former was the D32 unit, for direct assessment (by observation), and the latter the D33 unit, for assessment using diverse evidence (the portfolio). These have now been consolidated into a single unit of competence for assessors, the A1 Assessor Award.

Whether assessment is conducted by observation or examination of diverse evidence, it remains the responsibility of a single assessor. This means some sort of scrutiny, or moderation, of assessors' work is needed to ensure consistency, fairness and assessment to the correct standards. This is provided by verification, or the process of checking assessment. The awarding bodies that oversee the assessment and certification of competence-based qualifications (NVQs, and in Scotland SVQs) require two layers of verification: internal and external. Internal verification is carried out by an experienced assessor within the organization approved to offer the award, and initially has to cover 100 per cent of assessments, although this may be reduced once the organization has been assessing accurately for a while. External verification is carried out by the awarding body itself, on a sampling basis.

Illustrative example

A manager preparing for an NVQ in management may be required to demonstrate the competence 'Contribute to the assessment and selection of candidates against team and organizational requirements'. The assessor cannot realistically observe the manager conducting selection interviews, and so this competence is measured by diverse evidence. The evidence could include records that the selection interview took place, the manager's notes in preparing for the interview, the scoring sheet used to compare and select candidates, and perhaps a witness testimonial signed by the manager's co-interviewer. The assessor may need to interview the manager, to confirm that the evidence submitted is genuine and his or her own work.

NVQs, in the UK, provide a durable record of learners' competence, assessed to consistent standards.

FURTHER READING

Scott, J and Reynolds, D (2010) *Handbook of Workplace Assessment: Evidence-based practices for selecting and developing organizational talent*, Jossey-Bass, San Francisco

http://www.heacademy.ac.uk/assets/york/documents/resources/heca/heca_cl25.pdf (accessed December 2010)

http://www.qcda.gov.uk/, the website of the Qualifications and Curriculum Development Agency for England, Wales and Northern Ireland

72 Learning logs and contracts

As with assessment, the act of recording learning contributes to the learning process itself. There are many forms of learning record, including personal development plans, and portfolios of evidence, which are often used in conjunction with competence-based assessment. Here we shall concentrate on two kinds: learning logs, diaries or journals; and learning contracts, compacts or agreements.

Learning logs or journals are notebooks – or they could be online resources – where learners record their learning. This could mean simply noting what they have learnt, in an unstructured way, or it could be based on a template or formula, such as noting critical incidents or linking to a competence or assessment scheme.

The journal can help the learner to learn in a number of ways: by reinforcing the learning through the act of note taking itself; by offering opportunities for reflection when reading the journal; as a guide to action; and as a basis for discussion with other learners or with the learner's manager or support staff. The manager or support worker can help the learner by using the journal as a basis for coaching.

Learning contracts or agreements are documents drawn up between at least two parties, one of whom should be the learner. Other parties could be a coach or facilitator and the learner's line manager, among others. Contracts tend to be more structured than journals, as while the latter are retrospective accounts of what has already occurred (albeit for forward use too), the contract is a plan, or part of a plan, for future action.

The following may be among the features of a learning contract: a diagnosis of needs, specification of objectives, a plan for how learning will be carried out, identification of resources and sources of support, a timetable and milestones for meeting the objectives, and agreement regarding how the learning will be reviewed. As a contract, the document will require to be signed by the contractors. The formality of this tool appeals to many.

Written records help keep learning on track, and logs and contracts are different, but equally useful, means to accomplish this.

FURTHER READING

Anderson, G, Boud, D and Sampson, J (2004) *Learning Contracts: A practical guide*, Routledge, London

Boak, G (1998) *A Complete Guide to Learning Contracts*, Gower, Aldershot

Moon, J (2006) *Learning Journals*, Routledge, Abingdon

Nutley, T (2006) *Learning Log*, www.lulu.com

73 Guided reading

X-REF TOOLS

8 Informal and non-formal learning

16 The learning value chain

32 Personal development planning

56 Guided practice

Reading is one of the simplest – and oldest – ways of learning, or at least of acquiring information. Regardless of its limitations (see tools 16 and 56), it is a valuable part of the learning process. It is generally viewed as a solitary activity, and an overemphasis on it is seen as introspective, even antisocial, hence terms like 'bookish'. But it needn't be a solitary activity. Reading may be supported, may be a group activity and may be built into an organization's development plans.

The first thing an organization can do is hold a library of books and other reading material, and take subscriptions to relevant journals (both print and online). This implicitly encourages reading of the 'right' material.

The second thing is to organize reading in consultation with an individual. The reader and his or her manager or coach should agree a programme of reading, including a timetable, and arrange formal or informal sessions to discuss progress. The manager may discuss the content of the reading material, and how the reader reacted to it, and encourage application of the ideas in the reading to the work situation. This may be built into personal development planning, and form part of the performance and development review process.

Reading groups or circles allow small groups of learners to come together to discuss books they are reading at the same time. Members of the group provide a spur to other readers and help keep them motivated to continue reading. These groups may be facilitated by a senior manager or coach, or may be self-managed.

A simple formula for guiding reading, which works for both individuals and groups, is to:

- introduce the text;
- discuss the reading strategy;
- read (independently);
- review the reading;
- consider rereading if necessary, and review again;
- revisit the reading strategy and consider the next reading.

Overall, guided reading is a useful tool for making sure reading happens and for getting the best out of a common but sometimes disorganized practice.

FURTHER READING

The literature on this subject is mainly aimed at schoolchildren, and at adults with literacy problems, but the following may be useful: http://olc.spsd.sk.ca/de/pd/instr/strats/guided/guided.html (accessed December 2010)

74 Appreciative inquiry

X-REF TOOL

88 How to get value from learning consultants

Appreciative inquiry (sometimes abbreviated to AI, but not to be confused with artificial intelligence) is about positive change: it is a tool for organizational development that supports change management, renewal and performance improvement by building on the organization's culture and what is positive in what it already does and believes. As the term implies, it looks into what is happening in the organization in a way that is appreciative, and also relevant and collaborative, but still provocative. It is intended as the opposite of problem solving: instead of trying to fix things, it does not start from the assumption that things are broken or need to be fixed, but rather tries to build on what already works. The aim is to focus on strengths, not weaknesses.

The process for appreciative inquiry includes four phases, the 'four Ds' that form a continuous cycle. The discovery phase identifies existing organizational processes that work well; the dreaming phase imagines new processes that could work well in the future; the designing phase moves on to planning the processes that are agreed and identifying priorities; and the destiny or delivering phase implements the agreed design(s). This is represented in Figure 3.1.

Appreciative inquiry operates through a series of individual interviews and group meetings, with the findings collated into a report with conclusions and recommendations. This approach lends itself to the involvement of external consultants, but may also be facilitated internally.

FIGURE 3.1   Appreciative inquiry

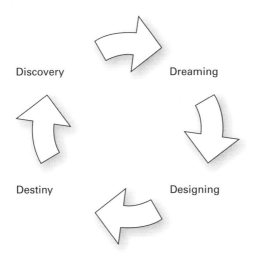

Discovery

Dreaming

Destiny

Designing

Illustrative example

The international banking crisis of 2007/08 left a major British bank in difficulties, having run up significant debts in its sub-premium mortgage lending activities and related hedge fund management operations. This led to that part of the business being separated from the rest of the bank, and prompted a searching review of the best strategy for the bank's core business in the future. Consultants were appointed to explore the parts of the bank that were stable, profitable and sustainable, and to make recommendations for future business development. Using appreciative inquiry, they were able to single out many strong aspects of the business, propose a vision to re-establish the bank's profitability and reputation, and in the process restore confidence and morale among staff, shareholders and customers. Appreciative inquiry helped show that, despite the problems and negative media coverage, the bank retained a sound, working business and good prospects.

FURTHER READING

Cooperrider, D, Whitney, D and Stavros, J (2008) *Appreciative Inquiry Handbook*, Berrett-Koehler, San Francisco
Stratton-Berkessel, R (2010) *The Appreciative Inquiry for Collaborative Solutions: 21 strength-based workshops*, Jossey-Bass, San Francisco
http://appreciativeinquiry.case.edu/ (accessed November 2010)

75 Networking via professional bodies

One of the best ways of informal and non-formal learning, and of continuous professional development, is through meeting with networks of other people, external to our own organizations, exchanging ideas and experiences with them, and maintaining contact with a view to future, perhaps mutual, benefit. This is broadly what networking is, and it is a vital learning and development tool.

David Clutterbuck (1998), in his *Learning Alliances*, singles out networking as one of a cluster of tools related to, among others, coaching and mentoring. The difference with this tool is that it looks to relative strangers to provide support to learners from their new experiences and fresh inputs.

Reduced to its simplest construct, networking is about little more than keeping in contact with others who may prove useful in future, but this is not to decry it. Networking can prove invaluable in expanding limited horizons, opening up opportunities for benchmarking, partnership or just sharing good practice, or for developing and cultivating contacts with a view to career development.

Professional bodies provide a forum for those who work in similar or related fields to network. Local branches hold meetings to introduce and bring together on a regular basis those who live near one another. Thematically linked groups help those with niche interests find like-minded others. The letters columns of professional journals offer scope for sharing written ideas, and online tools extend this much further (see tool 78).

Grades of membership with progression routes, continuous professional development schemes, regional, national and international conferences and gatherings, and other support mechanisms enable professional bodies to support their members to interact in many ways and to share their professional journeys. The learner who makes the most of the contacts and resources provided by professional bodies will learn more, and gain a developmental edge over colleagues who eschew these opportunities.

FURTHER READING

Clutterbuck, D (1998) *Learning Alliances*, CIPD, London
D'Souza, S (2007) *Brilliant Networking: What the best networkers know, say and do*, Prentice Hall, Harlow
Lindenfield, G and Lindenfield, S (2005) *Confident Networking for Career Success and Satisfaction*, Piatkus Books, London
Yeung, R (2009) *Networking: The new rules*, Marshall Cavendish, London
http://www.cipd.co.uk/
http://www.managers.org.uk/

76 Outplacement services

X-REF TOOLS

24 The succession planning cycle

64 Psychometric instruments for development rather than assessment

Outplacement is a tool an organization may use to assist individuals who no longer have a place within that organization move on to fulfilling employment or alternative career options elsewhere. This is consistent with planning how to develop and deploy talent, and with planning for succession, but acknowledges that there will be times when the organization is overstaffed or simply cannot afford to maintain previous levels of personnel. The sensitive nature of this subject means it is often described by a number of euphemisms, which only serve to confuse and don't really help anyone.

The process is typically facilitated by external agencies that offer corporate and private career consulting and outplacement services, although it is possible for organizations to manage it in-house. Such agencies, perhaps HR consultancies or niche specialists, offer a range of services from setting up in-house job or career centres for companies that may be shedding jobs through redundancies, to individual career reviews, counselling and career management programmes, perhaps for individuals looking to make a career move.

These services may also be accessed by private individuals but at a cost: employers are often looking for full value from career consultants and may be generous with the funding allocation, while individuals may be more cautious. People who have just lost their job and face an uncertain financial future may be sceptical about the value of intangible services like career counselling, where they can't necessarily see the benefit, but may be more receptive to more tangible offers like interview training or the creation of a new curriculum vitae (CV). In situations where the employer offers an allowance for outplacement as part of the severance package, individuals often decide not to use it in that way, preferring the cash alternative. However, where the employer retains career consultants to offer an integrated package, the uptake is usually very high.

The first stage in outplacement is often for a career consultant to be on hand when notice of redundancy is given, to make it clear that support services are available; failing that, the consultant ought to make contact as soon as possible to offer help.

The second stage is for the consultant to establish a relationship with the employee. This demonstrates the confidential nature of the work and helps get the employee settled. The use of objective data can help demonstrate that the employee's emotional experience is not unique, but is shared by most people who find themselves in that position. This is often the start of a series of face-to-face sessions between the consultant and the employee.

The stage that follows is to consider the individual's programme and make some decisions, such as agreeing the number of hours committed and how they will be spent. There is a range of inputs to discuss, and it is important to stress that the employee is going to have to do most of the work, and utilize the consultant's time as efficiently as possible.

Then the real work starts. The employee needs to look back and specify achievements, clarify knowledge and skill sets and, looking forward, identify career aspirations. Many people will be looking for a job, perhaps not unlike the one they have lost, but other options include consultancy, new business start-up or planning for retirement. Psychometric instruments can help individuals be clearer about what they need and what suits them best. The CV will need to be reviewed and redrafted. The employee will need to explore and better understand the job market. The consultant and employee will consider and agree a job search strategy and whether to use headhunters, online search methods, cold calling or other techniques, and decide on a job search campaign, essentially marketing him- or herself. The employee may need interview training, and certainly follow-up review meetings to analyse and assess progress.

A summary of the typical range of outplacement services is as follows:

- work in developing or improving CVs;
- work on covering letters to CVs;
- one-to-one counselling;
- group support work;
- the use of psychometric instruments;
- job interview training;
- provision of a manual of reading materials;

- provision of online support, such as a database of job search information or e-mail support;
- follow-up contact.

By developing people's interpersonal skills, with a focus on gaining new employment or an alternative occupation, outplacement is ultimately about helping people to help themselves.

FURTHER READING

Jones, E (1994) *Delivering In-House Outplacement: A practical guide for trainers, managers and personnel specialists*, McGraw-Hill, London

Lebo, F (1996) *Your Outplacement Handbook: Redesigning your career*, CRC Press, Boca Raton, FL

Morin, W and Cabrera, J (1996) *Parting Company: How to survive the loss of a job and find another successfully*, Harcourt Australia, Melbourne

Blended learning models

77

X-REF TOOLS

33 Using different approaches to learning and development
39 The five models of e-learning

Blended learning is a bit of a misnomer: it usually refers to blended *training*. Blending learning should really refer to what learners themselves do, regardless of the training methods deployed, when they opt in or out of aspects they like or dislike. However, the term remains a convenient shorthand to describe the approach to learning that involves combining online learning with offline learning, combining digital learning with non-digital learning.

In recent years, a number of different models of 'blended learning' have emerged; here are five of the most common:

- *The sandwich.* Perhaps the most common model is the course sandwich: this is what happens when pre- and post-course work is offered online. This is online learning with a 'traditional' face-to-face course as the sandwich filling. This offers learners choice and encourages transfer of learning.

- *The milestone.* Another classic form is to start with an online course and add on face-to-face training events (group work or one-to-one) as milestones, which help to pace the programme. This can help keep a group working to a set timetable, while retaining an element of individual flexibility as to what to study and at what time.

- *Knowledge-and-skill.* A third form is to use the online part of the blend for underpinning knowledge, while using a face-to-face approach for skill development. This is a cross-blend, compatible with both the sandwich and the milestone models.

- *Complementary resources.* A fourth form sees online learning resources offered as back-up to face-to-face training, allowing learners to refer back to coursework when they're on the job. In this form, the online part is subservient to the offline, but it's a blend that often works well.
- *The non-digital model.* A fifth form is not so new, and shows that it is perfectly feasible to have a blend that does not include online learning or indeed any digital technology. In the past this may have been referred to as mixed-mode or mixed-media learning, and could include any combination of face-to-face learning with print-based resources, audio and video technologies, and perhaps practical kits.

There must be many other forms, and many others may emerge as we become more adept at blending training inputs and learning resources.

FURTHER READING

Bersin, J (2004) *The Blended Learning Book: Best practices, proven methodologies, and lessons learned*, Jossey-Bass, San Francisco
Bonk, C J and Graham, C R (2006) *The Handbook of Blended Learning: Global perspectives, local designs*, Jossey-Bass, San Francisco
Littlejohn, A and Pegler, C (2007) *Preparing for Blended E-Learning: Understanding blended and online learning*, Routledge, Abingdon
Thorne, K (2002) *Blended Learning: How to integrate online and traditional learning*, Kogan Page, London

Social networking and collaborative tools

78

X-REF TOOLS

39 The five models of e-learning
75 Networking via professional bodies
77 Blended learning models

This could be described as the virtual equivalent of good old-fashioned networking; in fact, it is much more than that.

Social networking is conducted via a range of online tools for contact, discussion and collaboration. These have significant implications for how we manage many aspects of our lives, beyond the world of work, but have no less impact on ways of working. In a nutshell, social networking broadens the workplace to include regular contact and cooperation with everyone we know, and potentially with everyone everybody we know knows. Just as resources like Facebook have revolutionized our social lives, business networking sites like LinkedIn have empowered our work-focused networking.

More specifically, the collaborative tools that are the means of social networking have specific applications for learning and development, which bring this dimension into our learning interventions. The main tools to be aware of, and to use, are as follows:

- *Discussion forums.* In a discussion forum, any user can write and publish, or 'post', a new topic for discussion, and responses are shown within a discussion 'thread'. Thus learners may simply read discussion threads posted by others, or may choose to contribute to existing discussions, or may initiate new ones themselves, if they wish to become more active. Discussion forums are very common on many websites, quite apart from their use for learning, but have a mixed reputation, because some forums are underused, and when this is the case the application looks unimpressive. However, a well-used and well-moderated forum – moderators may prompt and guide discussions, merge related discussions, and move or delete inappropriate contributions – can be an invaluable learning aid.

- *Live chats.* One of the features of discussion forums is that the discussions take place asynchronously, with learners logging on and off when it suits them and contributing to the discussions accordingly. Live chat reverses this logic, and invites learners to contribute synchronously, or at set times, when they meet online to discuss things together. In every other respect, live chat works exactly like a discussion forum.

- *Podcasts.* Perhaps the least collaborative, these are audio or video clips that may be downloaded to a user's smartphone or handheld device. They may also, of course, be viewed or listened to on any computer. Podcasting can be seen as a much more targeted variant of more traditional broadcasting and, in a more interactive variant, allows a community of users the opportunity to publish their own podcasts.

- *Virtual classrooms.* These are comprehensive collaborative tools for staging interactive learning events online. A more detailed description may be found in tool 43.

- *Blogs.* These are like online journals, or logs, where the 'blogger' regularly writes and publishes – again, posts – his or her ideas and opinions. For learning and development, these can be useful for trainers providing ongoing information for learners, and the interactivity arises from the learners posting comments or questions to the blogger, which may lead to wider discussion. Learners can set up their own blogs, which can lead to extensive networking of blogs with related themes. Blogs offer scope for more directed variants of discussion forums. Micro-blogs, such as Twitter, offer scope for small-scale, and therefore much more frequent communication like this.

- *Wikis.* These are websites where users can share development of content and discuss their progress. The best known wiki collaboration is the worldwide, multi-language encyclopedia Wikipedia. The same principle is used to allow colleagues to share work documents, to develop learning content, including user-generated content, and to provide a means for learners to share contributions. This can work especially well in a blended learning context, where learners may want to exchange information after a face-to-face session.

New collaborative tools are emerging all the time. Learning and development professionals need to keep abreast of them and identify and utilize those tools that work best for the social networking they want to promote and for learning interventions in general.

FURTHER READING

Clapperton, G (2009) *This Is Social Media: Tweet, blog, link and post your way to business success*, Capstone, Oxford

Fraser, M and Dutta, S (2008) *Throwing Sheep in the Boardroom: How online social networking will transform your life, work and world*, Wiley, Chichester

Power, P (2009) *Know Me, Like Me, Follow Me: What online social networking means for you and your business*, Headline Business Plus, London

Richardson, W (2006) *Blogs, Wikis, Podcasts, and Other Powerful Web Tools for Classrooms*, Corwin Press, Thousand Oaks, CA

Vickery, G and Wunsch-Vincent, S (2007) *Participative Web and User-Created Content: Web 2.0, wikis and social networking*, OECD, Paris

http://en.wikipedia.org/

http://www.linkedin.com/

79 Checklist for setting up a learning centre

X-REF TOOLS

14 How to develop a learning culture

15 How to develop a learning organization

46 What to look for in learning materials

Learning centres, or learning resource centres, and their online equivalents, virtual learning centres, are facilities an organization can use to provide learning resources, coordinate use of them along with other learning activities, and act as a focus for encouraging a learning culture and building a learning organization. This sort of facility is more than a library, but less than a corporate university.

Perhaps the best advice to any organization looking to set one up is to visit existing and comparable facilities in other organizations and learn from their experience. There is also a body of theory to draw upon, and the checklist below distils some of the shared wisdom about setting up a learning centre. These are ten steps to follow:

1 Start by clarifying why the organization wants to have a learning centre. Is it to improve access to learning, or increase uptake of learning, or both? Does it need to provide a contact point for information and support for learning? Is the corporate rationale clear? Is there an explicit learning strategy, and if so how does having a centre fit with that? Will the learning centre have its own mission statement?

2 Think about the learners who will use the centre. Will it be solely for employees, or will it offer services to other stakeholders in the business, such as employees' families, suppliers and customers, or shareholders? Is any particular group a priority? Clarifying the user base helps clarify needs and therefore the centre's purpose.

3 Next, decide what sort of facilities and services the centre will provide. Will it offer quiet study space? Will it include print-based learning resources, digital learning resources, information about a wider range of learning services or support for other learning activities?

4 This brings us to the choice of learning resources. Which formats and which media will be used? Will there be objective selection criteria regarding style, relevance, whether the resources are up to date, etc? Who will decide which resources to acquire and how to do so? How will the inventory be managed?

5 Next, consider the provision of support to learners. Will support be internally or externally resourced, or both? Who will provide support? What sort of support – tutoring, mentoring, etc – will be provided? Will support be face to face, at a distance, technology supported, or a mixture?

6 Determine the staffing and resourcing of the centre. What staff will be needed? What facilities and what furniture and equipment will be needed? What sort of computer terminals and internet connectivity will be required? Or will it be a virtual centre, with no physical presence?

7 Consider the management of the centre. The success of a learning centre depends upon it being effectively managed. Aspects to manage include: staff; facilities; resources; technology; usage; support; linkage with other learning; evaluation; and marketing.

8 Consider the development of the centre. The strategy for it needs to go beyond initial set-up. How will the centre evolve? Will a planning cycle be followed? How will the centre be embedded in the overall organization? What are its goals and milestones beyond start-up? How will the centre be sustained long-term?

9 Consider the marketing of the centre. How will the centre be launched? How will it be promoted? Will the marketing mix include open days, promotional events, staff briefings, sponsorship, print-based publicity, online publicity, advertising, etc? How will its promotional activities be integrated with corporate marketing? How will it be clear whether the marketing is working?

10 Plan from the outset to evaluate and improve the centre. What will be evaluated and how? Will usage levels, user satisfaction, impact on learning, impact on individual job performance, or business results be evaluated? How can it be shown that the centre adds value, and how much value? Where will the evidence come from? Note that, although this is the last of the 10 steps, it is also a good place to start, and certainly plans for evaluation should be built in from the outset.

FURTHER READING

Malone, S (2003) *How to Set Up and Manage a Corporate Learning Centre*, Gower, Aldershot

Scott, A (1999) *Learning Centres: A step-by-step guide to planning, managing and evaluating an organizational resource centre*, Kogan Page, London

PART FOUR
Evaluating learning

This part of the book considers 21 tools that contribute to evaluation of learning.

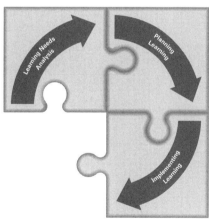

Costing learning 80

This is a template that may be adapted to help calculate the costs of any learning and development activity. Of course, every learning and development activity is different and carries with it different costs, so it is difficult to offer a blueprint for costing learning in any situation. However, Table 4.1 offers one standard scheme for weighing up the costs of a learning intervention before it is undertaken – or before any commitment is made to undertake it.

This template may be changed to address common costs in an organization by changing any of the categories in the left-hand column or adding to them. The last row should still offer a total and a cost per learner; adding up the figures in each column establishes the total costs for start-up and for ongoing delivery. Then dividing by the number of learners yields the cost per learner. Some organizations may already have their own templates; even then, this template may not be redundant, as it may offer a comparison.

The most substantial cost involved in many learning and development activities is the time of the learners themselves to participate in it. This is not covered by this template, but it may readily be calculated (and organizations often want to see this cost separately) by adding up the employments costs (salaries and related costs) for participating employees. This is not always the full story, though, as the opportunity cost, or replacement cost, of employees being away from their regular duties may be considerably higher than the cost of employing them.

TABLE 4.1 Costing learning

	Start-up costs or initial investment	Ongoing running costs
Staffing: Planning staff Managing staff Delivery staff Support staff		
Facilities: Premises/ accommodation Any alterations or adaptations Utilities Furnishings		
Running costs: Equipment (digital or otherwise) Telecommunications Learning resources Consumables		
Marketing: Publicity collateral Advertising/sponsorship Promotional events Staff briefings		
Other costs		
Total costs ÷ no. of learners = cost per learner		

This template is an elementary tool and, for large-scale or complicated learning and development plans, the support of accounting and financial analysis professionals will be required.

FURTHER READING

Lucey, T (2008) *Costing*, Cengage Learning, Andover
http://www.cipd.co.uk/subjects/lrnanddev/general/cstngtrain.htm, factsheet (accessed November 2010)
http://www.sil.org/lingualinks/literacy/planaliteracyprogram/ costingatrainingcourseorworksh.htm (accessed November 2010)

81 Assessing learning

X-REF TOOLS

48 Using qualifications

60 Preparing a lesson plan

71 Assessing and recording competence

90 Kirkpatrick's four levels of evaluation

A critical aspect of evaluating learning is to assess what learners have learnt; in Kirkpatrick's hierarchy, it is the second of the four levels. But its importance is even more fundamental: in any form of learning, a major interest is in what learners have actually learnt – some might argue it's the most important aspect of learning, albeit in learning for work we are also crucially concerned with the transfer of learning.

When planning to assess learning, there are seven key considerations to bear in mind:

1 *Assessment is itself a learning activity.* Anyone who has ever had to cram for an exam will recognize this: the process of exam preparation is often one of the best learning techniques. Assessment provides focus for learning, for the learner at least. This should be borne in mind when designing learning activities and assessment activities, and the two should complement one another.

2 *Assessment should begin with objectives and objective setting.* Just as the objectives describe what the learners should achieve as a result of the learning, so the assessment should show what they have actually achieved once they have completed it. This is enshrined within the learning and development cycle: for the individual learner, the identification of needs points towards the learning objectives, which are then defined when planning learning, and the fourth phase of the

cycle, evaluation, includes assessment of whether the learner has met the objectives.

3 *Make a distinction between judgement and scoring.* In practice the two are often conflated, and yet they are separate, albeit related, processes. When an assessor observes a learner carrying out a task under test conditions, the assessor first makes a judgement about whether the learner's performance is satisfactory, and then decides what score, or mark, to allocate to the learner. The more objective the assessment (see below), the less scope there is for the assessor to make a personal judgement, but the assessor still has to decide whether the learner has actually accomplished the objective(s). Scoring systems can allow for differentiation between the performances of different learners: both, or all, may be satisfactory, but some may be better than others.

4 *Utilize both formative and summative assessment.* Formative assessment is carried out to give feedback to learners and help them understand how they are progressing. Summative assessment is a kind of summing up, a means of assessing whether learners have fulfilled the assessment requirements, as may be necessary in order to confer an award or qualification, or to enable learners to move on to the next element of learning and assessment. The same assessment methods (see below) may be used for both formative and summative assessment: it is their use and context that make them different.

5 *Forget old notions about passing versus failing.* There are two kinds of scoring for assessment, norm referenced and criterion referenced. Norm referencing is where it is possible to be 'top of the class', as the comparison is with the performance of others. Its weakness is this: being the best bricklayer or the best salesperson in a company sounds good, but it depends how good the other bricklayers and salespeople are – if they are uniformly poor, it doesn't say much to be a bit better than them. Criterion referencing is where assessment is against a set standard or criterion. Being able to lay level bricks with even cement, of a specified number, within a required time, is a criterion-referenced measure of bricklaying. This has the advantage of being meaningful to someone else who may wish to employ a bricklayer, even if the person has no knowledge of how good the other available bricklayers are.

6 *Methods of assessment may be subdivided into three categories.* They are: assessment by one's self and the two kinds of assessment by others, subjective and objective assessment. Methods of assessment may be further usefully divided into clusters that address different skills and thinking, such as accessing information, problem solving, decision making, thinking critically, demonstrating techniques and, especially in the context of work, demonstrating retained knowledge and applying skills. Specific assessment methods may include:

multiple choice tests, true/false questioning, essays and other written work, work-based assignments, observation of work or simulated work, question-and-answer papers, portfolios of evidence and many more.

7 *Assessment must be subject to quality assurance (QA) or moderation or verification.* This is especially the case where the assessment is a matter of personal, subjective judgement, as it protects the learner against the mistakes or prejudices of an individual assessor, but it remains an essential discipline in all forms of assessment, as a means of ensuring checks and balances, not just to protect learners' interests, but to safeguard against plagiarism and other forms of cheating. QA is also a means of testing the reliability and validity of assessment processes: reliability is about ensuring consistency of assessment, and cannot be definitely tested, only estimated, but should be constantly checked in this way; validity is about ensuring the truth of conclusions in assessment, essentially checking their accuracy.

These seven considerations summarize the basics of assessment.

FURTHER READING

Cotton, J (1995) *The Theory of Assessment: An introduction*, Kogan Page, London
Gravells, A (2009) *Principles and Practice of Assessment in the Lifelong Learning Sector*, Learning Matters, Exeter
Wiliam, D (2009) *Assessment for Learning: Why, What and How?*, Institute of Education, London

Talent management and development: the GE nine box model

82

A key role for learning and development professionals in modern organizations is to plan and provide development routes for employees to fulfil not only their current roles, but the roles the organizations will need in the future. The nine box model is a tool for this, a matrix first developed at General Electric with McKinsey consultants, enabling employees to be assessed against the two distinct criteria of current performance (the horizontal axis in Figure 4.1) and future potential (the vertical axis). This tool is useful in identifying key talent, as well as in aiding the planning of appropriate learning and development interventions for the nine categories.

The terms used for each of the categories may be adjusted to the culture of your organization, as long as the underlying principle remains the same. For example, Andy Cross at Virgin Atlantic contrived to use the language of airlines ('turbulence', 'full throttle', etc), as cited in *The Talent Management Pocketbook* (2007).

A in the matrix represents those employees who show the best performance and potential and thus are staff to retain at all costs and earmark for

FIGURE 4.1   The GE nine box model

		below target	on target	above target
potential growth	*high*	**Maverick**	**Climber** **A/B**	**High flyer** **A**
		Problem	**Steady** **B**	**Rising** **A/B**
	stretch	**Risk** **C**	**Cruising**	**Solid**
		below target	*on target* **performance**	*above target*

greater things. More should be invested in their development, and they should be given more responsibilities and challenges.

B in the matrix represents those employees to retain if at all possible, give some priority to, and find ways to develop further.

C in the matrix represents those who currently are the poorest performers and have the least potential to improve. These employees need to be closely monitored and, if no ways can be found to improve their performance, ways will need to be found to manage them out of the organization.

The GE nine box model is a valuable tool, especially for medium to large enterprises or those that wish to take a thorough approach to managing the knowledge and skills of their workforce to meet organizational needs, both now and in the future.

FURTHER READING

Cross, A (2007) *The Talent Management Pocketbook*, Management Pocketbooks, Alresford

http://mkqpreview1.qdweb.net/Strategy/Enduring_ideas_The_GE-McKinsey_nine-box_matrix_2198 (accessed November 2010)

Quality management of learning: the diamond model

83

X-REF TOOLS

84 Applying quality management tools to learning
92 Measures in evaluating learning

This tool offers one possible model for quality management of learning.

Learning and development may be approached from the perspective of four strategic dimensions:

- strategy;
- resources;
- infrastructure;
- results.

This may be visually represented as a quality management (QM) diamond, with four dimensions within it, as in Figure 4.2.

The following is a list of 21 benchmarking statements, addressing each of these dimensions, which collectively may form the basis of a quality management system. The precise wording of these statements may not suit your particular organization and so may need to be adapted – one size does not necessarily fit all – but the general principles should be applicable to any context.

FIGURE 4.2 Quality assurance: the diamond model

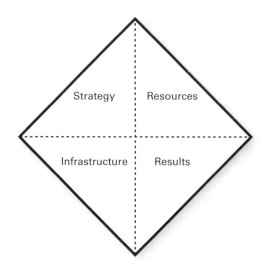

Strategy:

1 The organization has a written learning and development strategy.

2 Goals, values and commitment are expressed in the learning strategy.

3 The learning strategy is informed by learning needs analyses.

4 The learning strategy is informed by all relevant industry, professional and statutory requirements and recommendations.

Resources:

5 Appropriate equipment and technology are maintained.

6 All learning and development staff are suitably trained and qualified.

7 Budgets are in place to sustain ongoing learning.

8 Learner support is in place.

9 Learners have access to the best possible learning resources.

10 The organization maintains a database of all its learning provision, and relevant learning provision by suppliers and partners.

Infrastructure:

11 Reporting mechanisms are in place for learning, including regular monitoring and review of learning's effectiveness.

12 The organization has a coordinated approach to learning, with central control of learning strategy implementation.

13 The organization maintains records of all its learning activities.

14 The organization conducts regular assessments to match business needs with learning provision.

15 The organization links learning to its performance management system.

Results:

16 Where appropriate, off-the-job learning is linked to practical experience, to transfer learning to the workplace.

17 Learning is consistently delivered at an appropriate level to meet learning needs identified throughout the organization.

18 Learning provision fulfils the goals of the learning strategy.

19 Learning is regularly reviewed to ensure it meets industry and/or national standards.

20 There is evidence that learning provision has a positive impact on product quality and customer service.

21 There is evidence that learning provision saves on expenditure, increases revenue and/or increases profit.

Those responsible for implementing learning and development in the organization need to expand each of these statements to reflect the specific circumstances of their particular learning initiatives, devise means to generate evidence against each statement, and record performance to demonstrate quality. This then allows attention to focus on the areas of greatest variance.

FURTHER READING

The diamond model has been adapted from work originally developed in 2000 by the National Board for Nursing, Midwifery and Health Visiting for Scotland, now part of NHS Education for Scotland, available at http://www.qacpd.org.uk (accessed November 2010)

84 Applying quality management tools to learning

There are a plethora of different quality management systems and tools available that are relevant to learning and development. This is a quick summary of the range of tools not considered elsewhere in this book; each of them offers scope for reviewing and improving learning and development services:

- *Total quality management (TQM)*. TQM is an integrated scheme for continuous improvement of the quality of products, systems and processes. Its founding philosophy is that customers come first, and everyone should focus on the needs and expectations of their customers. Customers may be buyers or end users, but they may also be anyone in the supply chain that contributes to the satisfaction of the ultimate customer; hence we have internal as well as external customers. A less highlighted, but equally important, aspect of this is looking back through the supply chain to suppliers, and ensuring their needs and expectations are met. The roots of TQM lie in 14 principles of William Edwards Deming, which informed the practice of the Toyota Motor Corporation and others in Japan and worldwide, and influenced the concepts of just-in-time production, lean manufacturing and kaizen management, among others.

- *Baldrige criteria.* Malcolm Baldrige was a US politician who championed the US Quality Improvement Act of 1987. Named after him, the Malcolm Baldrige National Quality Award is an annual award in the United States that recognizes performance excellence in organizations in business, health care, education and charities. The Baldrige criteria are a set of 11 interrelated core values and concepts, which together form a tool for organizational self-assessment and self-improvement. The 11 are: visionary leadership; customer-driven excellence; organizational and personal learning; valuing workforce members and partners; agility; focus on the future; managing for innovation; management by fact; societal responsibility; focus on results and creating value; and systems perspective.

- *European Foundation for Quality Management (EFQM).* EFQM is a not-for-profit membership foundation based in Brussels, Belgium, and is the custodian of the EFQM Excellence Model, which offers a framework for 'sustainable excellence'. EFQM was founded in 1989 by 14 leading European companies to apply TQM with a European focus, motivated by a desire to improve Europe's competitiveness against the United States and Japan.

- *Investors in People (IiP).* IiP was launched in 1991 as an initiative of the UK government, and is a national standard for organizations to demonstrate their commitment to their employees, via a set of indicators such as 'Learning and development is planned to meet the organization's objectives', including evidence requirements such as 'People can confirm that their learning and development is planned to build their future capability to contribute to achieving the organization's vision'.

- *Other tools.* Other quality management tools for learning and development range from comprehensive systems like those above to simpler resources such as the seven basic tools of quality: the Ishikawa diagram; the check sheet; the control chart; the histogram; the Pareto chart; the scatter diagram; and stratification. Any or all of these may be useful to those who wish to manage quality in their learning and development practice.

FURTHER READING

Deming, W E (1992) *The Deming Management Method*, Mercury Business Books, New York

Hoyle, D (2006) *Quality Management Essentials*, Butterworth-Heinemann, Oxford

Liker, J (2003) *The Toyota Way: 14 management principles from the world's greatest manufacturer*, McGraw-Hill, New York

Oakland, J (2003) *TQM Text with Cases*, Butterworth-Heinemann, Oxford

Wood, J and Dickinson, J (2011) *Quality Assurance and Evaluation in the Lifelong Learning Sector*, Learning Matters, Exeter

http://asq.org/learn-about-quality/seven-basic-quality-tools/overview/overview.html (accessed December 2010)

http://www.baldrige.com/

http://www.efqm.org/

http://www.investorsinpeople.co.uk

Making a business case for learning and development

85

X-REF TOOLS

- **29** The six essential elements of a learning strategy
- **80** Costing learning
- **92** Measures in evaluating learning
- **96** Evaluation: return on expectations

Making a business case is about advocacy of learning and development, but most organizations have limited interest in rhetoric about how intrinsically good learning is; they prefer evidence to support their decision making, which is where evaluation comes in. In order to make a business case, it is necessary to have evaluation evidence that learning and development work.

Some argue that the case for a people-related service like learning and development is not the same as business cases for new product investments, but many of the issues are surprisingly similar.

A business case for learning and development, like any other business case, needs to be clear about its purpose: it needs to offer a clear recommendation, or set of recommendations, based on supporting evidence, with a clear analysis of the anticipated benefits for the organization, and it must be directed to those with the power to make the decision about whether to proceed.

Beyond these basics, the business case needs to have five clear characteristics:

1 It needs to have strategic alignment, which means it needs to be consistent with the organization's direction of travel, vision and values. It needs to fit into the big picture.

2 It needs to be based on robust needs analysis. There may not be evidence of past success, especially with something new, although comparisons with similar initiatives, or with the experiences of other organizations, may be useful. But it is always possible to provide analysis of needs, and precisely how the proposed solution(s) would meet them, perhaps with comparative consideration of the alternatives, including doing nothing. This may include a risks analysis, considering the consequences of not accepting the proposal.

3 It needs to be costed, in as much detail as possible. The decision makers need to know what they are being asked to spend, over what period of time, and from which budget. They also need to know the costs of alternatives.

4 It needs to be detailed, but summarized. This is not a contradiction: the decision makers need to be able to see that every detail has been examined, even if they don't have the time to scrutinize it all themselves. An executive summary enables them to cut to the chase.

5 It needs to meet the expectations of the audience (the board, or senior management, committee, etc). This means it needs to follow whatever format they are used to, and use the language they understand, and it needs to address their prime concerns.

Every business case will be different, but following the fundamental principles outlined in this tool should help ensure success.

FURTHER READING

Gambles, I (2009) *Making the Business Case: Proposals that succeed for projects that work*, Gower, Farnham

Pocket Mentor (2010) *Developing a Business Case*, Harvard Business School Press, Boston, MA

Schmidt, M (2009) *Business Case Essentials: A guide to structure and content*, Solution Matrix, Boston, MA

Internal marketing of learning and development

86

X-REF TOOLS

29 The six essential elements of a learning strategy
35 A checklist for procuring learning services
36 Outsourcing versus insourcing
85 Making a business case for learning and development

Learning and development professionals within an organization are often viewed by vendors as on the demand side of the market; in reality they are part of the supply chain, supplying learning and development services to their internal market within their organization. This sort of marketing work is something learning and development practitioners tend to underestimate, when in reality marketing is one of their most important activities.

The tool of internal marketing comprises two components, both borrowed from the marketing professions: segmenting and the Four Ps of the marketing mix.

Segmenting the internal market is about better understanding, and therefore better targeting, the internal market for learning and development.

The most common segmentation recognized and applied by learning and development professionals is by occupational type, such as managers, engineers, nurses, etc. However, there are other useful ways of segmenting the internal market. There is segmentation by customer objectives, where the learning and development function identifies customer expectations of the function and its services; there is segmentation by career categories, or talent clusters, which identifies important segments for succession planning or key talent development, such as fast-trackers; and arguably the most useful option is segmentation according to learning needs. The main drivers for segmentation by learning needs are issues like movement into new roles, organizational change, work improvements such as the introduction of new technology, and strategic business development.

There may be other possible segmentations in any organization, and analysis of them is always worthwhile: among other things, it helps determine how to deploy the other internal marketing component.

The marketing mix is often classified under the four Ps:

- product (or service);
- price (and opportunity costs);
- place (which is about distribution); and
- promotion.

- *Product.* Learning and development professionals need to reconsider continuously what their services are, and how these meet the needs of their market segments.

- *Price.* Thought needs to be given to costs and value (in comparison with those of possible external competitors), even if there is no formal mechanism for setting or charging internal prices.

- *Place.* In a learning and development context, this is not just about where to hold courses (although this can be important to learners) but about the use of other delivery methods, such as learning centres and e-learning.

- *Promotion.* This is about communicating effectively with all current and potential internal customers, in all segments. This requires some imagination and the use of a variety of techniques, such as advertising, publicity materials, promotional events, sponsorship or endorsement, and personal selling. Successful learning and development practitioners will place great emphasis on how they promote their services.

The crux of this tool is that learning and development practitioners should always consider their internal marketing from the standpoint that it is in direct competition with external training providers, because, whether there appears to be an immediate threat or not, that is always the case.

FURTHER READING

Ahmed, P and Rafiq, M (2002) *Internal Marketing: Tools and concepts for customer focused management*, Butterworth-Heinemann, Oxford
Linton, I (1997) *Marketing Training Services*, Gower, Aldershot
http://www.ebscohost.com/customerSuccess/uploads/topicFile-127.pdf (accessed November 2010)
http://www.trainingindustry.com/media/1590175/training%20efficiency-%20 internal%20marketing.pdf (accessed November 2010)

How to get value from a corporate university

X-REF TOOLS

14 How to develop a learning culture

15 How to develop a learning organization

22 The five aspects of talent management

43 What to look for in a digital learning platform

59 The seven pillars of a corporate university

Corporate universities sound grand, and may be attractive for their prestige value alone, but they can also be expensive to set up and run, so any serious consideration of them needs to be based on a clear understanding of how they add value to a business. There are nine distinct ways in which a corporate university (CU) may add value:

1 *By raising the profile of learning and development.* This is about more than simply raising awareness of learning and development. A properly organized CU, with a strong brand, should offer a greater sense of the place of learning and development. It should act as an incentive to employees to enrol on courses and enable people to see more value in learning.

2 *By conferring prestige on learning and development.* A CU doesn't just sound better: it can have a profound impact on how learners view the service. Learners should feel as though they are participating in some grand venture. Of course, it then becomes vital to follow through on that promise and ensure learners have memorable experiences, as well as learning that actually transfers to the workplace.

3 *By offering a clearer vision for learning and development.* Whether the CU has an explicit mission statement or not, it has to have a well-thought-through strategy and sense of purpose. The processes of building a business case, setting up a CU and launching it mean that people have thought about where it's aiming to be, demonstrably aligning employees' knowledge and skills with corporate objectives.

4 *By better organizing learning and development activities.* With centralized control, and a set curriculum, based on defined needs, a CU is better placed to direct and organize learning and development activities. A full complement of staff and resources will help with this. Better organization could also be accomplished by a well-organized, centralized learning and development function, not necessarily configured as a CU, but it should certainly be a consequence of doing things the CU way.

5 *By generating better information for reports and evaluation.* A further consequence of centralized control should be effective record keeping, which in turn should yield a better quality of information for reporting and to assist in the evaluation of learning. The CU collects all of the data that could be useful to the organization, both from the learning processes and from their outcomes, especially in terms of business results. It analyses that information and highlights the key points in reports to the relevant line managers, senior management and other stakeholders. A digital platform can help with this.

6 *By improving learner benefits, such as qualifications and professional development.* The CU should be primarily about achieving results for the business, and as part of that purpose it should also yield benefits for the learners, even if some of these are of no more than marginal interest to the business. Learners will be motivated by the learning itself, and by a sense of doing something useful for the business and getting better at their jobs, but they will also be motivated by personal achievements, such as qualifications, attaining milestones in their career development, and advancing in their professions.

7 *By helping to develop a learning culture, and to build a learning organization.* Many organizations talk about developing a learning culture and creating a learning organization, where learning is fostered as an integral part of business growth, yet they often lack any concrete initiatives to do so. The CU fills this gap. A high-profile CU, bearing the name of the organization, makes a powerful statement about the importance of learning in the organization, and offers learners the tools to develop themselves in a direction that helps the business.

8 *By providing a lever for talent management and other organizational development strategies.* A good CU is not an initiative that stands alone, or apart from other corporate initiatives: it should integrate with everything else in human resources and organizational development. Indeed, the CU can be the vehicle for delivery of other initiatives,

such as the learning and development requirements to fulfil talent management and development strategies. A well-thought-through CU will already hold records of learning needs and offer the courses and resources to meet them, and so is ideally placed to manage the outflow from organizational development strategies, especially when such strategies have foundered where ideas meet action.

9 *By contributing to a better corporate reputation, and promoting corporate values.* A good CU has the potential to have an impact beyond the traditional confines of HR and organizational development, and transcend the usual limitations of learning and development initiatives. This is because its brand and positioning lend it greater status in the organization. It can be adopted by senior management and shareholders as a symbol of the higher ideals of the organization; it can help make the organization a more popular place to work; it can attract external attention, publicity and awards; and it can help promote the values and aspirations of the organization.

These nine ways a CU adds value promise great returns, but they also represent a substantial investment of time and resources, and carry potentially significant costs. Nevertheless, the CU is not the sole preserve of the large corporation. The larger the organization, the easier it may be to establish a successful CU, but small to medium-sized organizations can also benefit and can also aspire to their own CU. Where potential learner numbers are very small, partnership working, such as with suppliers and customers, can help achieve the critical mass needed. Training vendors, or academic universities, or economic development bodies may be able to help bring together geographical neighbours, companies in the same sectors, or organizations with similarities but no directly competing interests. This may seem awkward, but the potential rewards could be worth it.

FURTHER READING

Allen, M (ed) (2007) *The Next Generation of Corporate Universities: Innovative approaches for developing people and expanding organizational capabilities*, Pfeiffer, San Francisco

Paton, R *et al* (eds) (2005) *Handbook of Corporate University Development: Managing strategic learning initiatives in public and private domains*, Gower, Aldershot

Walton, J (1999) Human resource development and the corporate university, Chapter 16 in *Strategic Human Resource Development*, FT Prentice Hall, Harlow

Wheeler, K and Clegg, E (2005) *The Corporate University Workbook: Launching the 21st century learning organization*, Jossey-Bass, San Francisco

88 How to get value from learning consultants

X-REF TOOL

45 What to look for in a learning and development consultant

Working with learning and development consultants can be very reward-ing, but it can also go horribly wrong. Identifying and engaging the right consultant is only the start of a process that needs to be followed through to ensure the organization gains the best value it can from the consultant.

The starting point is to choose the right consultant (see tool 45) and then continuously evaluate the consultant by considering the following 10 questions:

1 From the start, the organization may begin to test whether the consultant it thinks it engaged is the one it actually has. Are the consultant's credentials – claimed knowledge, skills and expertise – reflected in the way the consultant actually carries out the assignment?

2 As the contract progresses, does experience confirm that the consultant may be trusted to respect the confidences of the client organization? There is no room for compromise on this issue: if there is any evidence at all that the consultant can't be trusted this should be a deal breaker.

3 How well does the consultant focus on problems? Is the consultant adept at picking them out, adding value by identifying problems the organization didn't know existed, or does the consultant simply react to the client's prompts?

4 Does the consultant demonstrate clear differentiation of stages in problem solving, such as, to cite one model, problem identification, analysis, diagnosis and recommendations? These are key skills the consultant has been engaged for, and should be clearly evident.

5 Does the consultant report to the client regularly and clearly, in order to ensure the client is well informed of progress? This is something the client and consultant should have established together, but it can be encouraging to see the consultant being proactive on this.

6 Does the consultant form and maintain good working relationships with the client and all of the client organization's staff he or she comes into contact with? Good feedback from colleagues is positive, and complaints are negative, but these shouldn't always be taken at face value, as colleagues may have other agendas.

7 Is there evidence of the consultant effectively influencing people in the client organization? This means added value.

8 Does the consultant consistently adhere to contractual obligations, terms and conditions, and deadlines?

9 Does the consultant work to develop a legacy of independence for the client, as opposed to continued dependence upon the consultant?

10 Is the consultant open to having his or her performance evaluated, and does the consultant cooperate in such efforts?

Further questions may be added to reflect the specific requirements of the client organization and the particular circumstances of each consultancy assignment.

FURTHER READING

Cope, M (2010) *The Seven Cs of Consulting*, FT Prentice Hall, Harlow (to see things from the consultant's perspective)

Czerniawska, F and Smith, P (2010) *Buying Professional Services: How to get value for money from consultants and other professional services providers*, Economist Books, London

Perchtold, G and Sutton, J (2010) *Extract Value from Consultants: How to hire, control and fire them*, Greenleaf Book Group Press, Austin, TX

89 Evaluation: how to recognize and when to use the main methods

Evaluation is really a set of tools, but this summary represents a tool in itself, as it helps differentiate the main tools and suggests when each one may be appropriate. We need to differentiate Kirkpatrick's four levels, return on investment, return on expectations, Six Sigma, and total value add:

- *Kirkpatrick's four levels*. This is a classification of the kinds of things that may be evaluated in learning – reactions, learning, behaviour and results. Kirkpatrick's enduring idea, dating from 1959, was not just to distinguish the four levels, but to demonstrate that one can consider the impact of all training activities at each of these levels.

Kirkpatrick described these as four levels, rather than simply four discrete areas of measurement, because they form a hierarchy, from reactions up to results, in which each successive level benefits from information gathered at the level below. Thus Kirkpatrick's four levels represent not so much an evaluation method as a framework for a better understanding of what is being measured.

- *Return on investment (ROI).* This is an attempt to measure, in financial terms, the benefits from learning to the organization, which are essentially the increases in business value minus the actual costs of offering the learning. Cost–benefit analysis, which is essentially what this is, underpins many business decisions: identify and add up the benefits, identify and subtract the costs, and arrive at a measure of the return. By using division rather than subtraction, we arrive at a result that may then be expressed as a percentage: hence the formula in Figure 4.3. This simple equation is complicated by the need to measure return over time, leading to considerations of the payback period, and more robust (from an accountancy point of view) calculations such as net present value. ROI can be invaluable in converting ideas into tangible financial measures, but it may be compromised by benefits and costs being difficult to measure, calling into question the reliability of the figures.

FIGURE 4.3   ROI formula

$$\frac{\text{Total benefits}}{\text{Total costs}} = \text{ROI}$$

- *Return on expectations (ROE).* This attempts to improve on ROI by seeking to define the kind of value that matters most to the organization. Advocates of ROE propose defining the value that the customers of learning are looking for, and aiming to deliver that value. Critics of ROI describe it as a 'one-size-fits-all' approach and suggest ROE is more flexible. Some describe ROE as 'true ROI' (or TROI).

- *Six Sigma.* This starts from the same critique of ROI as ROE and argues that business measures, rather than training measures, are needed to convince customers of learning within any organization. Sigma is the Greek letter that, for statisticians, symbolizes standard deviation, a measure of variation; the number six derives from the number of process steps required to produce the Six Sigma goal of less than 3.4 defects (variations from the accepted standard) per million opportunities. Hence Six Sigma is the process whereby organizations improve quality by eliminating as far as possible deviations from the required norm. This approach is better suited to fixing existing processes (especially in a manufacturing environment) rather than identifying new products, services or processes. Arguably, it's more to do with efficiency than effectiveness.

- *Total value add.* This is an embryonic new approach, based on recognizing that many gains for an organization can be hard to measure in financial terms, including the benefits of advertising, brand value, goodwill, indirect benefits, intellectual capital, and more. This leads to the conclusion that evaluation of learning needs to embrace not just the financial return on investment, but an all-encompassing evaluation of all value added. Total value add is about using the ROE technique of clarifying what sort of value is most desired, about using ROI measures as well as others, and about building the case for learning on the accumulation of all the value it adds.

FURTHER READING

Anderson, V (2007) *The Value of Learning: From return on investment to return on expectation*, CIPD, London

Islam, K A (2006) *Developing and Measuring Training the 6 Sigma Way: A business approach to training and development*, Pfeiffer, San Francisco

Kearns, P (2005) *Evaluating the ROI from Learning: How to develop value-based training*, CIPD, London

Kirkpatrick, D L (1996) *Evaluating Training Programs: The four levels*, Berrett-Koehler, San Francisco

Ulrich, D and Brockbank, W (2005) *The HR Value Proposition*, Harvard Business School Press, Boston, MA

http://www.cipd.co.uk/subjects/lrnanddev/evaluation/evatrain.htm?IsSrchRes=1, factsheet (accessed November 2010)

Kirkpatrick's four levels of evaluation

X-REF TOOLS

89 Evaluation: how to recognize and when to use the main methods

91 Producing an evaluation sheet

Donald Kirkpatrick's four levels of evaluation, first expounded in 1959, remain, decades later, *the* big idea, the most significant contribution to theory of learning evaluation, despite many great contributions since. Kirkpatrick's four levels make a tool for better understanding what we are trying to accomplish in evaluation.

The four levels are: reactions, learning, behaviour and results, and these are depicted in Figure 4.4.

FIGURE 4.4   Kirkpatrick's four levels of evaluation

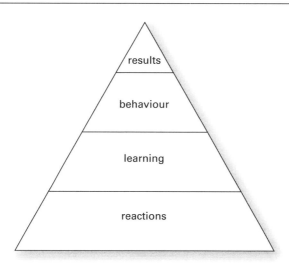

The reactions level, the lowest level, measures learners' immediate reactions to the learning experience, or their satisfaction with the learning. Whether the learning has been effective remains to be seen, but this level measures how happy the learners are or how they feel about the learning. This may be accomplished informally, via verbal questioning, or via the use of an evaluation sheet.

The next level up, the learning level, measures what learners have actually learnt, in terms of knowledge, skills and attitudinal change, as a direct result of the learning. This may be measured by examinations, skills tests, etc. In academic education, this could be the end of evaluation, but in occupational learning and development we are concerned with the transfer of learning to work: thence the remaining levels.

The third level, the behaviour level, measures the application of learners' improved knowledge, skills and attitudes to their behaviour in performing their work or, in other terms, the transfer of learning to work. This is harder to measure than reactions and learning; competence assessments are one way of trying to solve this problem, but the real challenge is to measure changes that take place in learners' work behaviour that may clearly be attributed to the learning.

The highest level, the results level, measures the gains the organization makes, or the business results, of the improved behaviour of the learners at work. This is the ultimate goal of the learning and, like the behaviour level, can be hard to measure: it is relatively easy to determine organizational performance metrics and track changes in them, but it is relatively hard to attribute these as direct consequences of learning.

The hierarchy, and how each level informs the next, is a source of some controversy. That the four levels are sequentially more sophisticated and yield higher-level (more valuable) information is not in dispute; what is questioned is to what extent they truly build upon one another – how much reactions inform learning outcomes, or how closely learning outcomes relate to business results. It seems reasonable to conclude that the hierarchy should not be taken too literally.

Over the years there have been various criticisms of the Kirkpatrick levels: ROI advocates have sometimes claimed ROI constitutes a fifth level, when it seems more apparent that it is a means of measuring level four; and Six Sigma advocates have dismissed the Kirkpatrick levels as insufficiently business oriented, which is hard to justify. Despite these criticisms, Kirkpatrick's four levels remain the most enduring tool for learning and development evaluation.

FURTHER READING

Kirkpatrick, D L (1996) *Evaluating Training Programs: The four levels*, Berrett-Koehler, San Francisco
http://www.kirkpatrickpartners.com/

Producing an evaluation sheet

91

> **X-REF TOOL**
>
> **90** Kirkpatrick's four levels of evaluation

For many people, the evaluation sheet, often mockingly referred to as a 'happy sheet', is as much as they will have ever encountered in the evaluation of learning. This is unfortunate: as Kirkpatrick has shown, this is the simplest, crudest measure of what goes on in learning and development, albeit a source of information fundamental to the higher levels of evaluation. Nevertheless, it is important that organizations get it right.

The evaluation sheet is known as the 'happy sheet' for two reasons: one is that it really only offers an immediate test of learners' satisfaction, or how happy they were with the learning; the second, more ominously, is that, owing to poor form design, it often yields only information that suggests learners are happy. There are two reasons why this may happen: one is if the person who designs the form is the same person who delivers the learning intervention and thus has a vested interest in the results; the second is due to common mistakes in drafting the form, which may be readily addressed by following the guidance here.

The golden rule in creating evaluation sheets is to keep them short and simple. It has been my misfortune to be involved in an evaluation exercise where the learners were expected to spend more time completing the evaluation than undertaking the actual learning. As a rule of thumb, the evaluation sheet should aim to fit on one page – two at the most. The questions it asks should be clear and unambiguous, and lend themselves to immediate responses – if the learners have to stop and think about it, it's not testing their immediate reactions.

The other important factor is about the kind of questions that are asked in the sheet. These should, of course, have an obvious relevance to the learners, but they should also be meaningful for those who will interpret the results.

There's no point asking questions about anything that can't be acted upon: the designers of the sheet should ask themselves what they will do if learners answer the questions in each possible way and, if there's nothing that can be done, consider whether the question is worth asking. A major part of the purpose of these sheets is to take corrective action where possible.

For ease of interpretation – and speed of response – it is a good idea to invite answers on a rating scale, often (and often mistakenly) referred to as a Likert scale, after the psychologist Rensis Likert. The scale is most commonly ranged over five standard responses, from 1, strongly disagree, through 2, disagree, 3, neither agree nor disagree, and 4, agree, to 5, strongly agree. Personally, I prefer to have an even number of responses, excluding the fence-sitting middle option: in my experience, responders will often create their own middle option anyway, but discouraging the neutral response yields more clear-cut data. Simple yes-or-no responses are even better.

Sheets may be designed on an alternative basis, such as a mind map, but this should only be used in exceptional circumstances or to make a change from the usual form if it has become mundane. Sheets should also, of course, test the suitability of the learning experience for those with special needs, and be available in alternative formats, such as large print, Braille or audio format for those with visual impairment. Web searches yield many templates for those reluctant to start from scratch, and these may then be adapted to take account of the issues covered here.

FURTHER READING

http://reviewing.co.uk/evaluation/evalform.htm (accessed December 2010)
http://www.technologystudent.com/designpro/eval1.htm
(accessed December 2010)

Measures in evaluating learning

92

X-REF TOOLS

89 Evaluation: how to recognize and when to use the main methods

94 Evaluation metrics

How well learning and development activities work may be measured in a number of different ways and against a variety of criteria. Table 4.2 provides a simple classification of the eight different kinds of measures that may be used in evaluating learning – there are two clusters of four, respectively absolute measures and comparative measures.

TABLE 4.2 Measures in evaluating learning

Absolute measures:	
Efficiency	This is a calculation of outputs divided by inputs, or benefits divided by costs, to yield the most efficient return, and drive the maximum gains for the minimum costs. Cost–benefit analysis, when both costs and benefits are expressed numerically, is a form of this.
Effectiveness	This means the sort of situation where outcomes are paramount and are not considered in relation to costs. Here, the driver is to achieve the best, or most effective, results, regardless of costs. Cost-effectiveness analysis, when costs are expressed numerically, but benefits in qualitative terms, is a form of this.

TABLE 4.2   *Continued*

Economy	Conversely, this is where costs are the overriding concern, and the measure is how low costs may go, or how inexpensive the learning could be (usually subject to the consideration that certain minimum standards must still be attained).
Value add	Like efficiency, value add is a measure of outputs versus inputs, but with the emphasis on the value added – in terms of knowledge, skills and behaviour – rather than costs.
Comparative measures:	
Baseline	This is a zero-based comparison, taking a starting point, or baseline, as the point of comparison. The baseline may not be zero, as it could also be a default or do-nothing comparison.
The norm	In comparisons with the norm, a measure can be taken against the typical or average performance, or a norm taken from a different historical period or work group.
Benchmarks	This is an external comparison, against another organization's performance, or perhaps against an industry sector average or a different but comparable industry.
Standards	This external comparison goes one stage further, and measures against occupational standards, or quality standards, or some other objective, well-established criteria.

These measures are not exclusive of each other: combinations of some may be used, particularly drawing one measure from each of the two clusters. There are many specific tools and metrics that may be deployed to achieve these measures, and these are the subjects of the remaining tools in this book.

There are also many different varieties of evaluation measurement methods. This subject is properly the preserve of research professionals, but learning and development professionals, or anyone involved in learning and development, may benefit from being acquainted with some fundamentals. Robson (2000) is one useful primer.

FURTHER READING

Robson, C (2000) *Small Scale Evaluation*, Sage Publications, London

CIPD partnership of learning model

93

The Chartered Institute of Personnel and Development's partnership of learning model is a holistic process focusing on value and aspiring to offer a new model of value and evaluation in learning.

Initiated in 2005, it gained momentum through a 'change agenda' paper written for the CIPD in 2006 by Valerie Anderson of the University of Portsmouth Business School, and it may be seen as a forerunner of, or contributor to, the return on expectations approach to evaluation (see tool 96). In citing research data that 80 per cent of learning and development professionals believe their efforts deliver more value than they are able to demonstrate, it also points to the total value-add approach (see tool 100).

The holistic dimension of the model is about a shift from learning activities and processes occurring in isolation, to those activities and processes becoming relevant to needs, integrated and aligned with the business of the organization, and continuous and ongoing. This requires all parties in the organization (and, in some cases, outside it) to be involved and to recognize and accept their responsibilities. This, for many, represents a significant cultural shift.

The partnership dimension is about close cooperation among four parties or partners: employers; line managers; individual learners; and trainers or facilitators. The model places all four partners at its heart, continuously exchanging information specifying what is needed, and delivering and validating learning.

What the partners deliver and validate is a series of objectives and outcomes, including: from the employer, alignment of business strategy with cost-effective collaborative learning; from the line manager, business benefits and improved organizational performance; from the learner, improved performance and development of job-related skills; and, from the trainer, effective and timely interventions to support relevant learning at all levels, utilizing frameworks, tools and resources.

The partners also provide processes and interventions to help specify needs, in the following roles: the employer expresses clear commitment to learning as a business driver and ensures that sufficient resources are made available; the line manager initiates opportunities for individuals to develop and apply their learning at work, and provides on-the-job coaching; the learner takes ownership and responsibility, seeks out relevant learning opportunities, and acts upon them; and the trainer supports, accelerates and directs learning interventions that meet organizational needs and are appropriate to the learner and the context.

Overall, this tool is about promoting a way of working that enables a culture shift from learning in isolation to relevant, integrated, continuous learning. This is one of the foundations of effective and meaningful evaluation of learning.

FURTHER READING

http://www.cipd.co.uk/NR/rdonlyres/5E28B57E-E9E1-4B19-ABA8-07DBBB6D07F3/0/MartynSlomanpresentationApril2008.pdf (accessed December 2010)

http://www.cipd.co.uk/NR/rdonlyres/94842E50-F775-4154-975F-8D4BE72846C7/0/valoflearnnwmodvalca.pdf (accessed December 2010)

Evaluation metrics

94

X-REF TOOLS

92   Measures in evaluating learning

95   Calculating return on investment

97   Six Sigma for learning and development

98   Balanced scorecard for learning and development

As in all forms of research, in evaluation there are quantitative and qualitative measures. The tools we use to implement the quantitative, or numerical, measures may be known as evaluation metrics:

- *Simple calculations* can yield many of the efficiency indicators we use in learning and development, such as numbers needing certain learning interventions, numbers registering for learning events, numbers attending, numbers completing, and the satisfaction scores from rating scales in evaluation sheets. Through collation of these calculations on spreadsheets, over time, a sophisticated picture may be painted of overall impact, and patterns within it.

- *Ratios* such as return on investment, return on assets, costs per employee and income per employee are important benchmarks for most organizations. Every organization will have key ratios that it constantly monitors as a guide to performance. The learning and development function needs to link into these calculations, and consider how learning and development affect these key ratios.

- *Cost–benefit analysis* is a metric for calculating the benefits of learning and development compared to the costs of planning and implementing them. Costs may be usefully distinguished between direct and indirect costs, and benefits may be distinguished between short-term and long-term benefits, and between easily quantifiable and hard-to-quantify benefits.

- *Break-even analysis* is the term for identifying the points at which benefits match costs – the break-even point, below which costs exceed benefits, and beyond which benefits surpass costs. By shifting some key variables, we can achieve break-even sooner or later, or influence where break-even occurs.

- *Cost-effectiveness analysis* is a metric for calculating how effective learning and development are, relative to costs incurred. As in cost–benefit analysis, this is a direct comparison, but a harder one to make, since measures of effectiveness are not so readily quantifiable. Often cost-effectiveness analysis seems incomplete, as it ends up with hard figures on one side of the equation and qualitative statements, even impressions, on the other.

- *Return on investment* is addressed in tool 95.

- *Six Sigma* is addressed in tool 97.

- *Balanced scorecard* is addressed in tool 98.

Despite (or perhaps because of) the large number of possibilities, learning evaluation metrics may sometimes seem to yield disappointingly few usable results. However, sometimes the journey is more important than the destination, and the process of enquiry and calculation itself can teach a lot about what has worked and what has had effect and meaning in learning and development. Even while answers remain elusive, evaluation metrics remain a valuable tool.

FURTHER READING

Phillips, J and Phillips, P (2009) *Metrics that Matter: What CEOs really think about learning investments*, ASTD Press, Alexandria, VA

http://www.training-evaluation-metrics.com/measure-most-important-training-ratios.htm (accessed December 2010)

Calculating return on investment

Return on investment, or ROI, is an established and reputable business tool beyond the realm of just learning and development. Finance and accounting professionals refer to the rate of return, or rate of profit, or simply the return, meaning essentially the same thing. The core concept is to measure the cost of implementing something, in our case learning and development, and compare that with the value generated for the business as a result.

In tool 89, we saw that cost–benefit analysis, which is the basis of ROI, underpins many business decisions: identify and add up the benefits, identify and subtract the costs, and arrive at a measure of the return. By using division rather than subtraction, we arrive at a result that may then be expressed as a percentage, hence the formula: total benefits, divided by total costs = percentage ROI.

The simplest way most organizations measure ROI over time is by payback. This measures how long it takes for the benefits to overtake the costs, and thus yields a payback period, or the time it takes to break even on an investment.

But the larger the investment, and the longer the period of time involved, the less accurate payback becomes. Accountants view payback as a rather crude measure, and seek more reliable, but more complex, calculation methods, including: the internal rate of return, or IRR method; the accounting rate of return, or ARR method; and discounted cash flow return, or the DCF method. Each of these takes account, in various ways, of factors like depreciation, allowance for inflation, opportunity cost of alternative investments, varying accounting conventions, etc. The most sophisticated, and most highly regarded, of these methods is net present value (NPV).

With NPV, effectively the return is adjusted to take account of capital depreciation, interest, vagaries of the firm's accounting practices and, perhaps most importantly, the effects of inflation. This means that a projected return, when looking ahead, is expressed in present day values or, in other words, adjusted to take account of the effects of inflation (and a retrospective calculation will use the actual rates of inflation). NPV is a useful tool, but only where the scale of investment justifies such a major effort of evaluation, as in itself it is costly and time-consuming, and many organizations that recognize the accuracy of NPV still prefer simple payback for practical working purposes.

In the calculation of ROI for a learning intervention, account needs to be taken of costs such as: trainers' salaries and expenses; hire of facilities and equipment; technology investments; external training providers' fees; administration costs; promotional costs; travel, accommodation and subsistence; and the salaries, as a measure of the lost work time, of the learners. There may be many others, depending on circumstances, and to give a true account everything should be considered to try to identify and calculate all costs. The benefits may be classified under headings like labour savings, productivity increases, cost savings, waste reduction, and whatever else may be important to an organization.

The strength of ROI is that is yields tangible measures, in pure financial terms, speaking a language that senior management understands. Its weakness is that it can represent an oversimplification, falsely reducing qualitative information to quantitative measures. Other controversies are whether it encourages short-termism, how reliable cost assumptions are in practice (and how open they are to manipulation to fit arguments), and how to decide what to measure, how to measure it and over what period. For some, these questions cast significant doubt over the validity of ROI measures. For others, these are practical obstacles to be overcome in pursuit of definitive evaluation measures.

FURTHER READING

Kearns, P (2005) *Evaluating the ROI from Learning: How to develop value-based training*, CIPD, London

Phillips, J (2003) *Return on Investment in Training and Performance Improvement Programs*, Butterworth-Heinemann, Woburn, MA

Phillips, P (2002) *Understanding the Basics of Return on Investment in Training: Assessing the tangible and intangible benefits*, Kogan Page, London

Phillips, P et al (2006) *The ROI Fieldbook: Strategies for implementing ROI in HR and training*, Butterworth-Heinemann, Oxford

Evaluation: return on expectations

X-REF TOOLS

89 Evaluation: how to recognize and when to use the main methods

90 Kirkpatrick's four levels of evaluation

92 Measures in evaluating learning

93 CIPD partnership of learning model

94 Evaluation metrics

While ROI starts from the assumption that everything can be reduced to a financial measure and therefore directly compared, return on expectations (ROE) takes the view that every stakeholder has different needs and expectations, and therefore evaluation should focus on what is most important for the stakeholder. Some advocates of ROE describe it as 'true ROI'.

ROE may be said to originate in academic work by Dave Ulrich and his collaborators in the United States, and has been developed and championed in the UK by the CIPD, based on research by Valerie Anderson and colleagues.

Among the key ideas underpinning ROE are:

- *Relevance*. What is the evaluation for, and why? Has work changed, and does the learning need to change?

- *Alignment*. Who is it for? Who are the stakeholders, has there been analysis of them, and have they been engaged?

- *Measurement*. What is the impact and value to be measured?

These may be distilled to a single fundamental principle of ROE, which is that value (which may or may not be capable of being reduced to a financial measure) needs to be defined in terms of customer or user expectations, and then that value has to be delivered, which means conducting some before-and-after measurements. A growing company that routinely delivers year-on-year sales figure increases may not be particularly impressed by learning outcomes that add one or two percentage points to the top line, but it may be extremely excited by learning outcomes that yield a tiny, beyond the decimal point, percentage increase to profits on existing sales, as this makes a much bigger difference to the company's bottom line. This example shows that clarifying expectations can make a significant difference.

ROE is another useful tool to deploy in evaluating learning.

FURTHER READING

Anderson, V (2007) *The Value of Learning: From return on investment to return on expectation*, CIPD, London

Ulrich, D and Brockbank, W (2005) *The HR Value Proposition*, Harvard Business School Press, Boston, MA

Six Sigma for learning and development

97

X-REF TOOL

89 Evaluation: how to recognize and when to use the main methods

---

Six Sigma is a different sort of tool for learning evaluation, in that it recognizes a need to take the perspective of the users of learning's outcomes. Six Sigma advocates argue that business measures, not training measures, are needed to capture the imaginations of learning's customers. Six Sigma has a different philosophical foundation, in that it sets out to identify and remove the causes of defects and errors, rather than simply to measure successes.

Six Sigma is a registered service mark and a trademark of Motorola Incorporated. One of the company's engineers, Bill Smith, is credited with inventing the tool in 1986, although some of its advocates claim to trace its history back as far as the 18th century. Sigma is the Greek letter that, for statisticians, symbolizes standard deviation, a measure of variation; in statistical process control, the number six derives from the number of process steps required to produce the Six Sigma goal of less than 3.4 defects, or variations from the accepted standard, per one million opportunities. Thus Six Sigma is the process whereby organizations improve quality by eliminating as far as possible deviations from the required norm. Motorola claims over $17 billion in savings in their first 20 years of implementing the process, and it is the cornerstone of Motorola University, widely recognized as the first corporate university in the world.

The adoption of Six Sigma by Jack Welch, when he was CEO of General Electric, led to a wider popularization of the technique, and some claim that it is now used, or has been used, by more than two-thirds of the world's leading companies.

The specification of 3.4 defects per million may seem an odd number, but there is a clear rationale. Sometimes people talk about 99 per cent accuracy as though this is an acceptable level, but in almost any business application it's not. One out of every hundred customer complaints is a lot to deal with, especially for a business dealing with a mass consumer base running into hundreds of thousands, and in dangerous work one fatality for every hundred employees is clearly an unacceptable level of accidental deaths. The figure of 3.4 defects in a million instances derives from the statistical improvements achievable at each sigma level up to six, and equates to 99.999 per cent accuracy, a far higher standard.

The application of Six Sigma to learning and development has been championed by Kaliym Islam, in his work at the Depository Trust and Clearing Corporation (DTCC) in the United States, and in his book *Developing and Measuring Training the 6 Sigma Way* (2006), which includes a case study of implementing e-learning the Six Sigma way at DTCC. Islam decries the instructional system design (ISD) approach – widely recognized terminology in the United States, but not really elsewhere – as divorced from business reality, and criticizes its theoretical forebears, including Donald Kirkpatrick, as ivory tower academics lacking business acumen.

The concept of ISD, especially the term 'instruction', jars with those of us who prefer learner-centred learning, as does Islam's preference for discussing training rather than learning. Perhaps the expressions of learning and development he has worked with are of the old, didactic style and, while his critique of that is more than justified, his conclusion of the need for Six Sigma represents a leap of logic, when other approaches address the same issues and are equally valid.

Islam recommends a model of Six Sigma called DMADDI, which he describes in six phases:

- *Define*. What are the business requirements?
- *Measure*. What targets do we need to meet?
- *Analyse*. What needs to be learnt?
- *Design*. How should we teach it?
- *Develop*. Does our prototype match our design?
- *Implement*. Did the implementation meet business and instructional requirements?

At the end of each phase in this process, a 'tollgate' review takes place, ensuring that the learning remains on track to fulfil business expectations, represented as the 'voice of the business' and the 'voice of the customer'. With Six Sigma, evaluation becomes an integrated activity with the rest of the learning or e-learning strategy. It becomes connected with the language and culture of the business. It should become not just more efficient, but more effective.

FURTHER READING

The discussion of this tool originally appeared, in a slightly different form, in Fee, K (2009) *Delivering E-Learning*, Kogan Page, London.

Islam, K A (2006) *Developing and Measuring Training the 6 Sigma Way: A business approach to training and development*, Pfeiffer, San Francisco

Balanced scorecard for learning and development

98

X-REF TOOL

84 Applying quality management tools to learning

Balanced scorecard is a tool for aligning learning and development (and other things) to the vision and strategy of an organization, improving communications, and monitoring organizational performance against strategy. It is an attempt to mix financial and non-financial information, to quantify qualitative measures and to produce an overall picture that is more helpful than other tools in guiding organizational decision making. Its origins have been traced to consultant Art Schneiderman, working at semiconductor company Analog Devices in the United States in 1987.

Its distinctiveness lies in identifying a small number of key measures – financial and non-financial – and attaching targets to them.

Following Kaplan and Norton (1996), most versions of the balanced scorecard identify four perspectives: the financial (derived from monetary measures), the customer (derived from perceived customer satisfaction), internal business processes (based on how the organization is structured and operates), and learning and growth (based on employees' levels of expertise). Then several targets, all of which must be specific and quantifiable, are set for each of these four perspectives.

The balanced scorecard is usually represented in four boxes, one for each of the four perspectives, as in Figure 4.5. Diagrams vary, depending upon how interdependent each of the perspectives is perceived to be, and there is consensus that there is some overlap, but there is no single definitive model of the tool. Some commentators distinguish different 'generations' of balanced scorecard, with the most recent having a more strategic focus, depicted in a strategy map. A deconstructed version applies a different balanced scorecard to different departments or functions within an organization, and aggregates these into an overall organizational picture.

FIGURE 4.5 Balanced scorecard

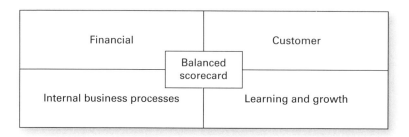

For those who find the classic – and simple – business model of raising income, reducing costs and improving profits too limiting, the balanced scorecard offers a way forward. By seeking to improve performance against each target for each of the perspectives, the balanced scorecard provides a cohesive tool for improving learning and development.

FURTHER READING

Kaplan, R and Norton, D (1996) *The Balanced Scorecard: Translating strategy into action*, Harvard Business School Press, Boston, MA

Pangarkar, A and Kirkwood, T (2009) *The Trainer's Balanced Scorecard: A complete resource for linking learning to organizational strategy*, Jossey-Bass, San Francisco

http://www.balancedscorecard.org/

http://www.training-evaluation-metrics.com/ (accessed December 2010)

E-learning: the impact matrix

99

X-REF TOOLS

38 The three component parts of e-learning

39 The five models of e-learning

The impact matrix is a tool I developed to evaluate the effectiveness of e-learning, and described in some detail in *Delivering E-Learning* (2009). It arose from a need I perceived to distinguish different kinds of e-learning (as in the five models in tool 39), but to try to do so in a more practical way, in terms that could be meaningful when applied to the particular circumstances of any organization. The explicit purpose of this tool is to measure the impact an e-learning implementation has, or could have, offering a comparison with other implementations.

In theory, at least, the impact matrix could be used to evaluate any learning and development approach (perhaps the use of self-study workbooks or other published learning resources, perhaps even traditional coursework), but the dimensions of the matrix have been chosen with key features of e-learning in mind, and these are not necessarily the key features of other learning approaches. By all means use it to assess other approaches, but please bear this caveat in mind.

E-learning, at least, can be differentiated along two lines, or axes: the generic–bespoke continuum and the knowledge–skills continuum. When we plot these against each other, we get the two-by-two boxes of the impact matrix. E-learning is often perceived as simply an online course providing information common to many contexts, sectors and organizations, but it can be a unique design, created exclusively for a narrow and particular group of learners: this is the generic–bespoke continuum. E-learning is also commonly associated with knowledge transfer, passing on facts, figures and information of a cerebral nature, and yet it is possible to develop e-learning that affords opportunities to practise and improve skills, especially skills involving the use of computers, but also anything that can be simulated using digital technology: this is the knowledge–skills continuum.

In the matrix depicted in Figure 4.6, e-learning that is more generic and more knowledge-based is represented by a cash cow: this is where the most widely recognized e-learning activity takes place, and is the main source of income for the biggest vendors of e-learning courseware. Hardly any vendors offer more skill-based generic courses, so that quadrant is represented by the question mark, as it remains problematic to see how that could work. More bespoke, knowledge-based e-learning is where organizations can get quick wins – and where many, especially low-cost, in-company initiatives are being forged – and this is represented by a star. But the toughest, most elusive, yet potentially most rewarding, e-learning to develop is bespoke e-learning with the capacity to develop skills, and so this represented by the holy grail.

FIGURE 4.6   The e-learning impact matrix

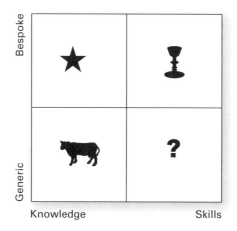

A test of the efficacy of the impact matrix is to place existing e-learning solutions within it and, if there are many, to look at the spread. Looking forward, it may be used to consider the likely impact of planned e-learning in an organization. Depending which type of solution is chosen, it is possible to predict with a fair degree of confidence the impact it will have, assuming it is well implemented.

Perhaps other impact matrices could be devised, for learning and development solutions other than e-learning, by choosing different axes.

FURTHER READING

Fee, K (2009) *Delivering E-Learning*, Kogan Page, London

Evaluation: total value add

100

X-REF TOOLS

21 Knowledge management: distinguishing data, information and knowledge

87 How to get value from a corporate university

89 Evaluation: how to recognize and when to use the main methods

Many gains for an organization are hard to measure in financial terms. The idea of total value add as an evaluation tool is to try to identify all of the gains and find ways to capture, measure and record them.

There's an old saying among marketing managers that half of their advertising budgets are wasted – they just don't know which half. Yet they continue to place advertising. This is an admission that they are doing something they are sure is of value, but find hard to justify based on the bottom line. Similarly, other aspects of an organization's work, such as brand values, reputation and customer or stakeholder goodwill, are difficult to place a monetary value on, in the balance sheet, but there is general agreement that they have some value, perhaps considerable value, although whatever figure is included may be a matter of guesswork.

This can apply directly to learning and development too. Sometimes learning and development activities have an indirect goal; sometimes they tackle issues like managing diversity to ensure equal opportunities for all employees, regardless of sex, ethnic origin or other diversities; sometimes learning and development may be undertaken because we fear the consequences of not doing it. All of this could be with a view to improving employee performance in the future, but would have no financial benefit as a direct result in the short term. Encouraging employees to develop the learning habit comes into the same category – enlightened organizations realize that, if their employees are keen to learn, it will be easier to implement change when required.

In short, there are many instances where gains to be made from learning interventions, or a range of other business activities, may be difficult or impossible to measure in financial terms.

Since the 1990s, organizations have increasingly become aware of their intellectual capital. This may be the most significant 'intangible' measure of business value yet. Thomas Stewart (1997) is among those who argue that the most important measures of value in a business are its knowledge assets, and that strategic development and deployment of these assets are the key to lasting competitive advantage, now and in the future. Stewart caricatures the work of corporate accountants as counting the bottles rather than describing the wine, and insists that it's the latter sort of value that is the 'hidden gold' of organizations.

What all of this – advertising and marketing, brand value and reputation, goodwill, indirect benefits, intellectual capital and more – bears witness to is that not everything can be reduced to a financial measure, and this is as true of learning and development as of anything else.

Total value add demands a wider lens than other evaluation tools, and is impossible to prescribe. Each organization needs to think creatively, organize brainstorming and other exploratory sessions, and work out what factors are being missed in current calculations. The list of items in the preceding paragraph is a start, but no more than that. This tool is about using the ROE technique of clarifying what sort of value is most desired, about using ROI measures as well as others, and ultimately about evaluating learning and development on the accumulation of all the value it adds.

FURTHER READING

Stewart, T (1997) *Intellectual Capital: The new wealth of organisations*, Nicholas Brealey, London

You

Finally, this is going to sound trite, but the single most important tool in your tool box is *you* – the person who is managing, implementing, delivering or supporting the learning. You need to be ready to confront every challenge as it arises, and so you have to prepare yourself.

Read. Study. Learn. Develop yourself. Solve problems. Gain experience of all sorts of different things. Think about things. Question your assumptions. Explore the unknown. Try to test out the tools and techniques you intend to deploy with other people, preferably on yourself first, if possible.

And this is not just about your motivation; it's about how you approach application of the tools. The wrong way is to look for opportunities to apply particular tools ('Where can I use accelerated learning?'); instead you need to have access to a large number of tools and know how best to apply the right tool when the situation arises ('Which tool will help me resolve this business problem?'). Your role is to match a tool to the situation, not the other way around – it's the situation that comes first.

The chances are you won't like every tool in this book: that's alright; you're not meant to. But it is hoped there will be tools you can find and use when you need them. You also can't expect to master all of the tools yourself, although you should hone your skills to excellence in a core set, but you should be in touch with other people who can help out when a different need is identified. The skill of deploying other people when appropriate is part of the value you contribute.

Make the most of yourself – you're the best asset you've got.

I wish you every success.

FURTHER READING

Pedler, M, Burgoyne, J and Boydell, T (2001) *A Manager's Guide to Self Development*, McGraw-Hill, London

INDEX